Routledge Revivals

The New Colonial Policy

The New Colonial Policy

Helmer Key

Routledge
Taylor & Francis Group

First published in 1927 by Methuen & Co. Ltd.

This edition first published in 2018 by Routledge
2 Park Square, Milton Park, Abingdon, Oxon, OX14 4RN
and by Routledge
605 Third Avenue, New York, NY 10017

Routledge is an imprint of the Taylor & Francis Group, an informa business

Publisher's Note
The publisher has gone to great lengths to ensure the quality of this reprint but points out that some imperfections in the original copies may be apparent.

Disclaimer
The publisher has made every effort to trace copyright holders and welcomes correspondence from those they have been unable to contact.

A Library of Congress record exists under ISBN: 27020841

ISBN 13: 978-1-138-60261-8 (hbk)
ISBN 13: 978-0-429-46211-5 (ebk)

THE NEW COLONIAL POLICY

BY

HELMER KEY, Ph.D.

TRANSLATED FROM THE SWEDISH BY

E. CLASSEN, M.A., Ph.D., M.R.S.L.

METHUEN & CO. LTD.
36 ESSEX STREET W.C.
LONDON

This translation first published in 1927

PREFACE

THIS volume, which I have called "The New Colonial Policy," incorporates material which has already been published in articles in the "Svenska Dagbladet" during recent years and which is now expanded and collated into a consistent whole. The book is intended as a continuation of my earlier work entitled "European Bankruptcy and Emigration." The purpose of the latter was to show that it was beyond the bounds of possibility to pay international war debts and to extort vast reparation sums from Germany, as was at first intended. In my opinion there existed no other rational solution than the organization of a considerable volume of emigration to transoceanic lands in order to create new markets for European exports. Only in this way was it possible to restore the economic equilibrium which existed before the war between Europe and the transoceanic continents. Since my last book was written the realization of the impossibility of accomplishing a full liquidation of war debts and reparations has been more commonly appreciated and great efforts have been made to arrive at a rational solution of the problem. The Dawes plan has been devised to solve the problem of German reparations, but the question of the regulation of international debts remains still in the main unsolved. Similarly it would appear extremely doubtful whether the large transfer of capital to various countries, as contemplated by the Dawes plan, is feasible in practice. The Dawes plan may for a time disguise the general bankruptcy, and it may be presumed that at least for the time being it may produce one good effect: that of gradually educating future opinion in the knowledge that the payment of international debts and reparations is on the whole impracticable.

The important question of sufficient emigration from Europe to transoceanic lands remains as insoluble as ever. The purpose of this new book is primarily to bring up to date the account of the world position which was the foundation of my previous book. It also deals more exhaustively than the previous volume with the problem of European over-population. In the latter connection a number of other closely related questions are discussed, such as a more suitable distribution of the population of the earth over its various continents and the much discussed question of birth-control.

HELMER KEY

STOCKHOLM
May, 1927

CONTENTS

THE NEW COLONIAL POLICY

CHAPTER I

THE POVERTY OF EUROPE

The Economic Equilibrium between the Continents of the World

BEFORE the Great War there existed between the various continents a division of labour which favoured the economic progress of the world. In some respects this balance was perhaps more apparent than real, but the main thing was that people believed it to exist. Then, as now, there existed keen international competition, but it was not so devastating, and it had rather a stimulating effect on the productivity of the different countries.

One of the conditions precedent of this relative equilibrium in world economy was a constant emigration from Europe to oversea countries. Emigrants, mostly agricultural labourers, settled in suitable districts and contributed to the increased production of the raw materials and foodstuffs required by Europe, and exchanged for the products of European industry. The consequence was that the price of oversea goods gradually fell, but not so far as to make continued production unprofitable. The buying power of the oversea countries increased and rendered possible an increased consumption of the products of European industry.

Here and there, it is true, industries grew up on a more or less modest scale in oversea countries, but with the exception of the U.S.A., which occupies a special position, these new industries did not seriously compete with European goods, which were of better quality and in greater demand in proportion as prosperity increased and civilization advanced among the colonists and coloured races. This moderate industrialization of oversea countries had scarcely any other effect than to contribute to the raising of the standard of living in such countries, for example, as India, Japan, the Argentine, and Brazil. This in its turn tended to increase the effective demand of the world. In other words, equilibrium existed between the production of raw materials in the colonies and the steadily increasing output of European industry.

Since the war conditions have entirely changed. Purchasing power has been diminished throughout the world, with the exception of the U.S.A., and this is due to the fact that the equilibrium between production in Europe and in oversea countries, which was based on normal emigration from Europe, has been destroyed.

This disturbance has been intensified by the over-industrialization of Europe caused by the war and its aftermath, a process in which the essential feature is that factories in many important branches of industry have developed a technical capacity which far exceeds the demand for the goods which the world market can absorb.

In consequence the price of colonial raw material and foodstuffs rose at the same time as the price of European industrial products fell. European industry was compelled, therefore, at a time when demand was reduced, to work with dearer raw materials and higher costs of production, the latter as a result of a higher cost of living and higher real wages.

At first the inflation of paper currency in most European countries had a stimulating influence on industrial production, but it soon appeared that this was only a passing phase. The turnover appeared very great owing to high prices, but the increase in value did not correspond to any increase in quantity. On the contrary, the volume of world trade shrank considerably, and the shrinkage was world-wide.

It is also quite natural that the worst effects of the economic developments after the war should be found in Europe, especially in Central Europe, where the position was rendered still more difficult by certain Draconic and impracticable provisions of the treaties of peace.

Enterprising spirits in different countries established, in the years immediately succeeding the war, new undertakings without any regard to costs of production. They counted upon a progressive currency devaluation, and all sorts of speculators in inflation eagerly sought to satisfy their hunger for material values by buying shares in such undertakings. Accompanying this movement there arose in almost all European countries an effort to emancipate themselves as far as possible from dependence on foreign sources of supply. Instead of the special subsidies which many industries enjoyed during the war, high tariffs were introduced.

"The system of self-contained trade states," said the Austrian Secretary of State, Dr. Elemer Hantos, in an article in the "Neue Freie Presse," which gives an excellent and comprehensive survey of the situation after the Great War, "began to reassert itself, aided by political unrest. Not a few undertakings arose as a direct consequence of the treaty of peace. By separating districts economically and geographically one the conditions precedent for the industrial development of Central Europe were changed. The peace treaty suppressed from the uniform organization certain links in the chain of production, and the new distribution of territory created the necessity for replacing them by others. Large factories found themselves situated in small countries without any market therein, and every state endeavoured within its own frontiers to create as quickly as possible an organization which, in relation to foreign states, would work as satisfactorily as before the war. Factories which had formerly produced for the whole of the Hapsburg monarchy found themselves compelled to abandon their principal works and instead to split up their activities among the various succession states. Tchek, Austrian and German textile mills placed capital in new factories in Hungary, and in Austria were founded china and glass factories in order to make those countries independent in this respect of Tcheko-Slovakia. Poland endeavoured to create within its own factories large-scale manufacture in a number of branches and on a scale which was disproportionately great."

"From an economic point of view," continued Dr. Hantos, "this development has been extremely unsound and has compelled large concerns to work at a fraction only of their potential capacity, whilst such articles as they formerly produced are manufactured in new factories in neighbouring states. It was the peace treaties, protection and inflation which together brought about this result."

Hantos' utterance is in fact a confirmation of the economic consequence of the peace treaty which Keynes foresaw in his work on "The Economic Consequences of the Peace," in which he prophesied the fatal effects which must follow, especially in Germany, from the sundering, by new frontiers, of the old economic unity.

Broadly speaking, the inflation crisis lasted until 1923. After that date began the stabilization of currencies which avenged the earlier unsound and exaggerated consumption. Production had to be restricted, but the new and extended factories remained. The whole of this vast new apparatus was all the more precarious since the productive capacity of the Central European industrial states after the war was already much too great in proportion to the reduced volume of world trade, then reckoned at about 50 per cent. of the pre-war volume.

As has been said, this development appeared unfavourable not only to Europe, but also, to some extent, to oversea countries, in so far as they found it more difficult to sell their raw materials. This fact gave rise in the years immediately succeeding the war to an economic crisis, the effects of which are only now being overcome. The only exception is the U.S.A., which only profited by the war and thereby greatly increased its purchasing power and national revenue. The effect of this state of affairs is injurious to Europe, which in consequence has become heavily indebted to, and financially dependent upon, the U.S.A.

The situation is rendered still worse by the fact that Europe is even more dependent upon the supply of foodstuffs and raw materials from oversea countries than before the war, as may be seen, for example, in respect of imports of grain. Yet another consequence of the war was that oversea countries, which were unable to procure European manufactured goods during the war, began to erect their own factories to produce them. This tendency to industrial autonomy in the colonies and oversea countries is for Europe one of the most serious economic phenomena of the post-war period.

Europe can no longer lay claim to the economic and industrial hegemony which it possessed before the war. Its supremacy has vanished, and in proportion as power slips into the hands of other continents, Europe's material and moral position must be weakened. It is manifest that this decline has already begun. Europe is no longer, as in the last century, the principal manufacturer and banker of the world, i.e. the market in which the best goods were made and in which foreign exchanges were regulated.[1]

Europe imported in the nineteenth century raw material from the so-called " new " countries and exported these raw materials in the form of manufactured goods. This special position of Europe was based on two things. Firstly, the existence of coal, which was, so to speak, the bread of industry; and, secondly, the scientific technique, which is the spiritual foundation of the whole of modern economic development.

An energetic drift towards economic independence of Europe is to be found nowadays not only in autonomous oversea states such as the Latin republics in South America and Mexico, but also in almost all the great British dominions such as India, Australia, South Africa, and Canada.

In Australia there exists an economic imperialism which has found consistent political expression. One may point to the establishment of a special Ministry of Trade and Industry with its subordinate Bureau of Science and Industry, and to the tariff

[1] Cf. Etienne Antonelli: "Les destins de l'Europe," "Revue Economique Internationale," pp. 421 *et seqq.*

legislation which appears to become more and more protectionist with each year that passes. The changed position in Australia is also reflected in the changed distribution of the population as between urban and rural areas. In 1901 the population of Australia was 3,773,000, but by 1921 it had risen to 5,435,000. Simultaneously the rural population had fallen from 32 per cent to 25 per cent. of the total. The proportion of industrial workers had increased from 20 per cent to 26 per cent. During the same period the number at work on the land had, it is true, increased from 533,107 to 598,675, but the number employed in industry had increased still more, from 426,166 to 723,559.[1]

A similar development may be seen in the Union of South Africa. In 1916 the Union Government established a special industrial bureau with an Advisory Committee, and in 1917 a special Federation of Industries was established for South Africa. Statistical investigation has shown that during or after the war there have been erected within the Union not less than 4,047 new factories, with a combined capital of £45 millions sterling.

A similar development, though even more comprehensive, is visible in British India, where not only the cotton industry, which has old roots in the country, has greatly developed, but also the iron industry has been expanded by undertakings of great magnitude. As an example may be mentioned the

[1] Etienne Antonelli, *vide supra*, pp. 431 *et seqq.*

Tata Iron and Steel Company, with a capital of 140 million rupees and an annual production of about 700,000 tons of pig iron. This concern is the more remarkable as it was established entirely on native Indian capital. Another similar undertaking was established in 1921 under the name of the United Steel Corporation of Asia, Ltd., with a capital of 200 million rupees. The Indian Government was compelled for domestic reasons to favour such a development. In 1921 was founded the Central Department of Industry, and in 1922 the Indian Store Department, an organization founded to promote the purchase of home-made goods instead of imported goods. It follows as a matter of course that Indian policy, like the Australian, is taking a more and more protectionist direction.

A similar development is taking place in the Argentine, in Brazil, and in Japan. Especially the countries on the Pacific littoral are taking steps to safeguard their special interests, and in the same year as the Treaty of Versailles was concluded the Pan-Pacific Union was formed by Alexander Hume Ford with the object of achieving economic cooperation among the countries round the Pacific Ocean.

CHAPTER II

THE ECONOMIC EXPANSION OF TRANSOCEANIC COUNTRIES

Development at the Expense of Europe

IT cannot be denied that from an economic point of view there are many natural reasons for the endeavour of the transoceanic countries to liberate themselves from the economic hegemony of Europe. It is intelligible that one should seek to transplant the manufacturing industries to those parts of the globe where the raw materials are obtained or where the cost of living is low. In many cases there is also the further advantage of locating an industry in the place where its output is actually consumed. One cannot close one's eyes to the fact that a pair of shoes made in London of Australian leather and subsequently exported and sold in Sydney must be dearer than the same pair of shoes made in Australia. The same applies to cotton goods. It must be cheaper to manufacture on the spot cotton clothes intended for sale in India or Egypt instead of first sending the raw cotton to

Europe to be worked up there. In this connection it should be noted that it is not always advantageous to work up the raw materials in the place where they are produced. The necessity of importing raw materials may be counterbalanced by other favourable factors such as expert labour, low cost of living or hereditary skill. Thus, for example, the renaissance of modern Italian industry is undoubtedly to be attributed to such special conditions as those here referred to. Broadly speaking, however, it is true that no power on earth can resist a development which aims at the transplantation of industry to the most natural sources of production,[1] and in the long run it is probable that Europe must accommodate itself to the altered economic position which must ensue. But this does not prevent Europe from seizing every available means to maintain its position in those fields where the natural conditions are favourable, and above all from putting forth all its energy to prevent the economic hegemony passing into other hands by default. In this case we must think primarily of the danger threatened from the United States.

The colossal advance made in the U.S.A. at

[1] In exceptional cases it may of course happen that, as a result of climatic or other conditions, the production of, for example, certain "quality" goods is more suited to Europe than anywhere else, even though raw material must be imported. This happens, for example, with the textile industry in Lancashire, the high quality of which is due to especially favourable climatic conditions.

present exerts very severe pressure on Europe for various reasons, but especially because Europe is heavily indebted to the United States, which, after the war, possessed more available capital than any other country. Moreover, the United States have increased the volume of their turnover not only with all European states, but also with practically all oversea countries, in which they advanced during the war at the expense of Europe and conquered markets which Europe is seeking at great pains to recapture.

Further striking evidence of the decline in the economic position of Europe is to be found in the development of the mercantile tonnage of the world. According to Lloyd's Register the mercantile tonnage of the world in June 1925 amounted to 64·6 million tons gross, corresponding to 49·1 millions in June 1914. England's mercantile marine in June 1925 as compared with 1914 was almost stationary, and amounted to 19·4, as compared with 19·3. Germany had lost about 2½ million tonnage. The U.S.A. had increased its tonnage from 5·3 to 15·4, Japan from 1·7 to 3·9, and the British Dominions from 1·8 to 2·8 million tons.

These statistics do not in themselves sufficiently illuminate the position if one also takes into consideration the profit-earning capacity. It is well known in what a miserable financial position the more or less State-owned American shipping finds itself. American competition can only be maintained by great sacrifices on the part of the American State. But even if this constitutes a burden on the American taxpayer, it yet does not prevent the American competition being extremely injurious to Europe. In the year 1913 there were only 11·4 per cent of imports into the U.S.A. carried in their own bottoms and 9·1 per cent exports. But in 1920 the corresponding percentages of the foreign trade of the U.S.A. had risen to 42 and 43·6 per cent. This increased use of American tonnage has taken place at the expense of other nations, and of course principally to the detriment of European ship-owners, and this in its turn has helped to increase the adverse balance of Europe.

Wherever one turns in the economic field, it becomes more and more clear that the feeding of Europe is dependent on oversea countries. This may be clearly seen in the case of grain, for example, in the developments in 1924–5, the years during which Russia completely disappeared as a grain-exporting country. In the autumn of 1924 there occurred a great rise in the price of wheat, combined with a bad harvest in Canada and a moderate harvest in the U.S.A.

An interesting survey was published in "The Economist" on 27th December 1924, which showed that the area under wheat cultivation in Europe had decreased, whereas in oversea countries it had progressively increased. Expressed in millions of hectares the world's cultivation of wheat averaged in the years 1909–13 in comparison with 1924 as follows.

	Average Area. 1909–13.	Average Area. 1924.
Europe (except Russia)	29·3	26·5
U.S.A.	19·1	21·8
Canada	4·6	9·8
India	11·8	12·6
Argentine	6·5	7·2
Australia	3·1	4·0

The procuring of raw materials for the textile industry introduces another field in which Europe's dependence on countries outside of Europe is very striking. Outside the U.S.A., which is at present the most important producer of cotton, and where the textile industry has flourished for a long time, many other cotton-growing countries have begun to manufacture for themselves. As a set-off to the cotton production of the U.S.A. new plantations have been established in other places, such as Egypt, China, East Africa, Brazil, and Mexico, but of these Egypt is the only one deserving serious consideration. In the others the production of cotton is too inconsiderable in comparison with that of the U.S.A.

In other countries cotton production is still comparatively insignificant in comparison with the production of the U.S.A. The difficulties of European manufacturers in procuring sufficient raw material in years of poor cotton crops have been increased by the great prosperity of the United

States, in so far as they themselves require a large part of their crop. Until the end of 1926 prices were maintained above the pre-war level, but as a result of the record crop of that year a great fall in prices occurred in the U.S.A. In 1913 the crop amounted to about 14,000,000 bales, in 1923 to only 10,000,000 bales, but the November estimates for the 1926 crop amounted to 18,000,000 bales, from which it is clear that a considerable quantity of the crop must be held over until 1927. The annual consumption of the U.S.A. is estimated at about 15,000,000 bales, but as there is already a large surplus stock, it is calculated that on the 1st of July 1927 there will be an available surplus of 7,500,000 bales for U.S.A. use or for export. Every fall in price is of course an advantage to the European market. The cotton must, however, always be purchased from oversea countries, and whenever there is any stringency Europe must pay large additional sums for its supplies. The following particulars of prices on different occasions will suffice to show what vast sums are involved. In 1913 the average price paid in Liverpool was 7*d.* per lb. The highest post-war price was reached in January 1924 at 19·3*d.* per lb. In January 1926 the price had fallen to 10·7*d.* per lb., but on 23rd November of the same year the price was down to 6·93*d.* per lb., i.e. below the pre-war price.

Similar conditions have prevailed in the wool market, in which prices soared tremendously after the war. The highest prices were obtained in 1924, when Australia was unable to cope with the increased demand, and although prices have fallen somewhat, yet wool quotations in the middle of 1926 were considerably higher than before the war. The average 1913 price in Bradford per lb. tops was 20*d.*, corresponding to 25·8*d.* in April 1926, and the quotation for merino tops was 30*d.* in 1913, as against 51*d.* in April 1926, per lb.

When the price of such articles of consumption as wheat, wool and cotton rises, Europe becomes incapable of producing suitable goods in exchange. The most important goods of this kind are potash and dyestuffs, but it is obvious that it is easier to restrict the consumption of articles not necessary to the maintenance of life than to restrict the consumption of foodstuffs such as wheat, or textiles such as cotton and wool.

In the matter of textiles, Europe has recorded one point to its own advantage in the last decade. Variations of price may be occasioned by other causes than increased or decreased production. They may also result from new inventions. In this category must be included the production of artificial silk, which has increased enormously in recent years. The production of natural raw silk increased from 1913 to 1925 by 69 per cent, but the production of artificial silk increased by no less than 560 per cent. Expressed in tons, the world production of artificial silk amounted in

1913 to only 14,000 tons, but in 1925 to no less than 92,000 tons. In proportion as the use of artificial silk displaces cotton and wool, the advantage must be on the side of Europe, as three-quarters of the world output of silk is produced there. The remainder is produced in the U.S.A., though Japan also contributes not inconsiderable quantities.[1]

Other important raw materials which Europe is obliged to import from overseas are rubber and copper, though the prices of these commodities had sunk below the pre-war level even earlier than the prices of cotton. Standard copper was quoted in London at the average price for 1913 at £68·3 per long ton, corresponding to £57·3 in April 1926, and rubber (standard ribbing smoked sheet) at 38·3*d*. per lb. as the average price for 1913, and 25*d*. in April 1926.

Rubber is the only tropical product of which the cultivation is still controlled by Europe.[2] Before

[1] "Memorandum sur la production et le commerce," Société des Nations, Section Economique et Financière, Genève, 1926. This memorandum, which I have also had occasion to quote in another connection, constitutes a part of the preliminary studies for the international economic conference which it is proposed to hold in May 1927. The initiative in this work was taken by a preliminary committee consisting of three well-known economists, i.e. Dr. F. Hodac, General Secretary of the Tcheko-Slovakian Federation of Industries, W. T. Layton, Editor of "The Economist," and Professor Allan Young of Harvard University.

[2] See further, *inter alia*, Alfred Vagt's "Kautschukpolitik, Zeitschrift für Geopolitik," Aug. 1926, pp. 631 *et seqq*. Jacob Viner: "National Monopolies of Raw

1900 almost the whole of the world's rubber was produced in Brazil, where it was tapped from virgin trees, principally in the primeval forests of the Amazon. But at this point English capitalists began to interest themselves in rubber cultivation outside the tropics, and this movement to produce raw rubber developed very rapidly. In 1914 the quantity of plantation rubber exceeded for the first time that of natural rubber. In the beginning of the 'twenties plantation rubber yielded over 90 per cent of the whole of the world's production. The quantity was more than five times as great as had ever been obtained from the natural supplies. The consequence was an over-production of plantation rubber, which produced a considerable fall in price, as mentioned above, and it began to look as if this cultivation was doomed, owing to intense internal competition.

The British Colonial Office then instituted an inquiry by the so-called Stevenson Committee, which in 1921 submitted a report on raw rubber production in the colonies. This report concluded with a proposal for the regulation of production, by which it was hoped to stave off ruin from the plantations. The basis of the proposal was that each producer should restrict his output to a so-called "standard" quantity. The actual produc-

Materials," Foreign Affairs, July 1926, pp. 568 *et seqq.* Harry N. Whitford: "Rubber and the Philippines," *ibidem,* July 1926, pp. 677 *et seqq.*

tion of the year 1920 was taken as the basis in calculating this quantity. Every producer was to have the right at first to export from his plantations 60 per cent of the standard quantity. The Colonial Secretary accepted the proposal and issued an order, on 1st November 1922, regulating production in those colonies cultivating rubber. The plan came into force in the first quarter after the issue of the order. At the end of each succeeding quarter the export quota was to be raised above the quota for the immediately preceding quarter by an amount equal to 5 per cent of the standard quantity, provided that the price in the preceding quarter had been maintained between 1*s.* 3*d.* and 1*s.* 6*d.* per pound, and by 10 per cent if the price had exceeded 1*s.* 6*d.* On the other hand, if the price fell below 1*s.* 3*d.* in the preceding quarter the *quantity* must be reduced by 5 per cent

Export was to be regulated by means of licences. If a producer violated the order and exported more than he was licensed to do, he was subject to severe taxation on the whole of his exports. The order was obeyed not only by planters in the British Colonies, but in the Dutch Indies also English planters voluntarily submitted to it.

The intervention of the Colonial Secretary saved the British rubber plantations, but it cannot be said that England's position as the owner of a world monopoly of rubber production was thereby strengthened. The restriction of export from the

British rubber plantations had the result that new plantations arose in districts not subject to British rule, and especially in the Dutch Indies. British control, which in 1922 was effective over 72 per cent of the world's production, sank in 1923 to 63 per cent, and to an even lower figure in the succeeding years. According to statements in the July number of "Foreign Affairs," and the August number of "Geopolitik," the world export of rubber during the last seven years was as follows (net export in tons):

Before Control.	British.	Other Countries.	Total.	British Share, per cent.
1919	257,484	91,090	348,574	74
1920	226,081	78,590	304,671	74
1921	200,959	75,787	276,746	73
1922	271,589	106,643	378,232	72
After Control.				
1923	237,434	142,304	379,738	63
1924	205,027	181,676	386,703	53
1925 [1]	302,983	200,184	503,167	60

It is to be noted, moreover, that the production of raw plantation rubber has begun in various places, independently of Europeans, by natives. This occurs especially in the Dutch Indies. In these colonies the question of legislative safeguards is mooted in order to protect the native plantations and to stimulate the natives to further efforts. This production of raw rubber, which is naturally

[1] The figure for 1925 is not fully comparable, as it also includes the production of natural rubber.

outside the restrictions of the English Stevenson plan, has already assumed alarming proportions. According to "De Indische Mercuur" [1] the export of dry rubber, which in 1921 was only 6,000 tons, amounted in 1925 to no less than 80,000 tons, with an estimated value of 250 million Dutch florins. About 80 per cent of this production comes from the provinces of Djambi and Palembang in Sumatra, and from districts in the west, south and east of Borneo. The journal quoted expresses the belief that this production can be doubled in the near future.

Plans are also being made to erect factories to work up this raw rubber, in order that it may be exported direct to consuming countries instead of, as at present, being sent to Singapore factories for treatment.

It looks as if the Dutch Government had the intention of promoting the erection of such factories in the Dutch Indies, whilst at the same time seeking to control production in order that these may be assured of a sufficient quantity of raw material, without unsound competition. Undoubtedly the phenomenon of the production of raw rubber on the initiative of the natives of the Dutch Indies is a remarkable sign of the times. It constitutes one of the many proofs that developments are at present unfavourable to Europe and the white races, and are to the advantage, not only of over-

[1] "De Indische Mercuur," 7th July 1926, p. 518.

sea countries, but also of their coloured populations.

Although England has not succeeded in acquiring the entire world control of plantation rubber, yet its position, even after the Stevenson restrictions, was so strong that it occasioned great anxiety in the U.S.A. and evoked there a violent campaign against English interests. The attack was led by the then Minister of Trade, Hoover, who maintained that Great Britain had arrogated to itself a world monopoly in raw rubber, to the injury of world trade, and especially of U.S.A. trade. Hoover declared that the situation was all the more dangerous for the United States since those States were the world's largest consumer, consuming alone more than 70 per cent of the world's production. The U.S.A. could therefore not consent to be dependent on England. Diplomatic representations were made to the British Government on the ground that England had permitted "combinations in restraint of international trade." Naturally the British Ambassador in Washington repudiated most firmly this accusation. It was maintained both in the Press and elsewhere that the highly protective tariff legislation of the U.S.A. occasioned even greater restraint of international trade. Meanwhile the agitation in the U.S.A. was kept alive, and the American Government sought to turn it to advantage by stimulating American raw rubber enterprise.

In the summer of 1925 Mr. Harvey Firestone, president of the Firestone Tyre and Rubber Company in Akron (Ohio), sought to obtain a concession of 1,000,000 acres in the negro republic of Liberia, which is under strong American influence. It was calculated that this concession would be large enough to create a rubber output sufficient to make the U.S.A. independent of Great Britain.

The effect of the Stevenson control has been that in recent years the world consumption of raw rubber has exceeded the production by about 150,000 tons. If the British colonies were to produce at full capacity, it is estimated that the whole rubber area under cultivation in the East could meet the world demand during the years 1926, 1927 and 1928. From and including 1929 it is assumed that consumption will exceed production. It takes five years for a rubber tree to begin to yield and eight years before its yield reaches the maximum. As things now stand there is the possibility that in 1933 the world market will require 150,000 tons more raw rubber than can be obtained from present sources of supply. The Americans must, therefore, if they wish to participate in the control of the production of raw rubber, prepare to meet this estimated increase of consumption in the beginning of the next decade.

The only districts under American political control which possess favourable climatic conditions for the production of rubber are the Panama zone and the Philippine Islands. The district around the canal zone must be thoroughly prepared to be of use, and the possibilities of cultivation there will always be limited. The highest imaginable yield is estimated at only 10,000 tons per annum. Much more favourable are the conditions in the Philippines. It is supposed that there are there not less than 1,500,000 acres of soil suitable for rubber growing on Mindanao and other neighbouring islands, and it is calculated that the yield might be forced up to about 200,000 tons annually. But conditions in the Philippines do not attract American capital. The restrictive legislation on the islands in reference to the ownership of land by foreigners constitute a great obstacle, to which must be added that the inhabitants are not well disposed to American investments on a large scale, as they see in them a political danger. The present dependence on the U.S.A. is not popular; on the contrary, leading opinion in the Philippines demands complete political independence. All these circumstances have combined to scare away American capital, and it seems improbable that Americans will risk large investments in the Philippines unless there should be a considerable restriction of the present relative independence of the islands.

At the moment of writing there is a report in the Press that the Philippine Parliament is said to be considering a Bill to facilitate the leasing to foreign companies of land suitable for rubber plantations. Companies whose share capital is owned as to 61 per cent by American or Philippine citizens are to have the right to lease a maximum of nine estates of 50,000 acres each for a period of seventy-five years. The estates must be separated from each other by a distance of at least one English mile. Whether this proposal, if it becomes law, is sufficiently attractive to encourage Americans to invest more largely than hitherto in rubber plantations in the Philippines remains to be seen.

The Hoover campaign has not succeeded in bringing about on any large scale American investment in rubber plantations. The Liberia scheme has not yet materialized. It has been the object of criticism, and it has been urged as a warning that Great Britain failed in its attempt to plant rubber in Liberia. Moreover, it would be very difficult to attract in the United States the immense capital required for the realization of the projected enterprise. Americans do not like to invest in undertakings with a slow return, as is necessary in rubber companies. Americans like to reap their gains quickly, or, as the president of one of the largest American rubber companies expressed himself, "In this country we live next to the 'ticker,' or 'tape,' which brings in the latest stock quotations."

The American Government has continued its

agitation and has succeeded so far that it has, at least on paper, brought a couple of undertakings into existence with the object of founding American rubber plantations with American capital "in a big way," as the phrase is. The first of these, the American Motor Rubber Corporation, was founded on the 12th January 1925, on the initiative of the National Automobile Chamber of Commerce, of which nearly all U.S.A. motor-car manufacturers are members. The company was started with a share capital of 12 million dollars. A few days later a company of the same kind, and with even larger pretensions, was founded in connection with the New York Motor Show. A project was presented for the formation of a Rubber Association of America to protect the American public and the rubber industry with respect to future supply. The scheme embraced the next five years and assumed an annual contribution from the Association of 10 million dollars for the promotion of American rubber plantations. Hopes were held out that State support would also be forthcoming, but it is not yet clear whether the proposal has led to any practical result. To all appearances the Americans still display no special enthusiasm for direct investment in tropical rubber plantations.

On the other hand, it would appear that the English are still making great efforts to retain their monopoly, which, even if it is only comparatively effective, must yet be counted of considerable value both for Great Britain and for Europe. One often reads in the Press new accounts of the expanding interests of the English in rubber. Thus, for example, they have bought from the Danes a large rubber plantation in Sumatra, a concern of about 8,000 cultivated acres, belonging to the Danish-East Indian Plantation Company. The Danish owner of the majority of the shares was the Aarhus oil works, and the purchase price is reported to have been 10 million crowns.[1]

From the above it would appear that, at least up to the present, Europe has succeeded in retaining the leading position in the world production of raw rubber.

An extremely important economic factor is coal. Before the war, Europe was the principal seller of this raw material, but nowadays it experiences difficulty in finding an export market. The causes are various. Other fuels, such as oil, have begun largely to replace coal, and hydro-electric power has come into much more general use, especially in railway locomotion. In respect of oil fuel one may especially point to the increased use of oil firing or oil motors for propelling ships. Ten years ago there were scarcely any oil-fired vessels, but according to Lloyd's Register for

[1] There exists in Sumatra another Scandinavian rubber plantation, but this comprises not more than 1,200–1,500 acres. The interested parties in this plantation are said to be principally Norwegians.

1925–26 the world's tonnage consisted of steam and motor vessels totalling 597 million gross register tons, of which 17·8 millions were oil-firing and 2 millions oil motors. And it must be remembered that this development is still in its infancy.

In addition, coal-getting has been taken up on an ever-increasing scale outside Europe. Already in 1916 Mr. D. A. Thomas, later Lord Rhondda, stated in the House of Commons that Great Britain could not expect to retain its monopoly of coal production in the future, as many coalfields existed in other parts of the world, which had not yet been exploited. When they came to be worked the market for British coals must necessarily decline. This development was hastened by the World War. Great Britain had difficulty during the war in providing its earlier customers with coal, with the result that the latter were compelled to supply themselves with suitable fuel from other sources, and in many cases availed themselves of their own, hitherto unexploited, supplies.

In the beginning of the nineteenth century the output of coal in the world was 12½ million tons, of which England alone supplied 10 million tons. Even up to 1890 England was the leading nation in respect of coal, but in the year 1923 the U.S.A. produced 50 million tons of coal a month, whilst England did not produce more than about 25 million tons in the same period. Other countries, such as Japan, India, Canada, and South Africa, also began to produce coal, and have attained quite considerable quantities. In Great Britain the output of coal in 1925 was less than one-fifth of the world's production, whereas in 1896 it provided a third, and in 1870 not less than one-half.

The decline in England's oversea coal exports is striking. In 1913, England exported to Brazil 1,900,000 tons, but in 1924 not more than 800,000 tons; to Uruguay, 723,000 tons in 1913 and 419,000 tons in 1924. To Egypt were exported in 1913, 3,100,000 tons, but in 1924 only 1,800,000; to Chile in 1913, 600,000 tons, but only 19,000 tons in 1924. In some of the above cases the decrease in Great Britain's exports is due to the fact that the purchasers have begun to exploit their own coal mines.[1]

[1] As was pointed out in connection with the production of rubber, it is possible that we are on the eve of a revolution in respect of coal and oil in the event of the successful solution of the problem of extracting oil from coal by the Bergius process.

CHAPTER III

RAW MATERIALS AND TRADE

Some Post-War Views

THE world position in respect of the production of raw materials and the international exchange of goods has been exhaustively studied in the above-mentioned memorandum of the League of Nations on finance and trade.[1]

In this memorandum certain points of comparison between pre-war and post-war conditions are set forth, in which the investigation is restricted in the main to the changes which have occurred since 1916 in regard to :

The population of the earth and its distribution ;

The production of raw materials and foodstuffs in the world as a whole and in its various parts ;

The volume and geographical distribution of world trade.

The following summary shows the relative size,

[1] See also "Svenska Dagbladet," "Världsproduktion och Världshandel," by Ansgar Rosenberg, 20th November 1926.

raw material output and international trade for 1925, compared with 1913, for which the basic figure is 100:

	Population.	Raw Material production in percentage of 1913.	International Trade.
Europe [1]	101	105	89
North America	119	126	137
Central America [2]	107	171	128
South America	122	135	97
Asia	105	124	136
Africa	107	139	99
Oceana	116	124	132
Whole world	105	118	105

The production of foodstuffs and industrial raw materials has increased more rapidly than the population, and foreign trade was probably greater in volume by 16–18 per cent in 1925 than in 1913, despite the fact that in the latter year production was greater than in any other year before the war. But it should be noted that the index numbers for Europe are lower than those for the rest of the world. North and Central America, Asia and the South Pacific islands have increased both their import and export trade. The total trade of South America and Africa has somewhat diminished, but that of Europe has decreased far more. European exports in volume had fallen in 1925 by 20 per cent in comparison with 1913.

[1] Including Russia.

[2] Including Mexico and the West Indies.

North American (the United States and Canada) export trade has increased since 1913 by almost a third, and Asiatic trade in an almost equal proportion. From this the conclusion may be drawn that even if the centre of economic activity is still to be found in the North Atlantic, yet there is a strong tendency for the centre of gravity to be shifted in favour of the United States and Japan.[1] This development points to the development of a new centre in the Pacific, which constitutes a connecting link between North America on the one hand and the Pacific coast of Asia and the rich East Indies on the other.

Despite the fact that the value of the world's trade has increased between 50 and 60 per cent, yet European exports from 1913 to 1925 have only increased by about 32 per cent. It is therefore clear that economic developments are proceeding much more rapidly in other continents than in Europe. We may also note the changes, arising from disturbances in various groups of commodities, which at the same time point to changes in consumption consequent on an altered average standard of living throughout the world. From these changes it appears that the production of vegetable foodstuffs has relatively lost ground, whilst the production of the raw materials for clothing, paper and

[1] Cf. Helmer Key : " European Bankruptcy and Emigration," Methuen & Co., Ltd., London, 1924, pp. 38 and 41–55.

luxury articles has gained ground. These changes are in the main the same as those which occur in ordinary family budgets when the income is increased, and point to the raised standard of living throughout the world during the years succeeding the war. But as the facts of the situation in Europe point to an average *status quo ante,* it is clear that this raising of the standard of living is principally to the good of the other continents.

It cannot be denied that the report contained in the League of Nations Memorandum affords interesting statistical data, but scarcely sufficient material for a reliable estimate of the economic position of the world. Various objections to its conclusions have been raised by, among others, Professor Gustav Cassel,[1] who points out that the capacity of the colonies for producing raw materials and foodstuffs is not so limited as has sometimes been supposed. From this fact he concludes that we cannot *prima facie* attribute the bad economic situation in Europe to insufficient development of the extra-European output of raw materials and foodstuffs. It appears, moreover, from what has been said above, that the tropical products which rose so unreasonably in price during the war and the succeeding years of crisis, have now sunk to a level which is in some cases even considerably lower than before the war. At the same time, as

[1] See "Svenska Dagbladet," 17th and 20th December 1926.

Professor Cassel points out, the prices of European manufactured goods have generally risen, so that in April 1926, for example, the Swedish price index-number for manufactured goods was 155. Broadly speaking, therefore, Europe should import raw materials from the colonies more cheaply than before the war, whilst prices of manufactured goods are as a rule above the average. Europe, therefore, is in a position to obtain a larger quantity of raw materials and foodstuffs for a given quantity of manufactured goods than before the war. That Europe nevertheless experiences difficulty in selling its manufactures must be primarily due to the fact that Europe produces too little and at too high a cost, with the result that in spite of the fall of prices Europe cannot procure as many colonial products as are to be desired. Europe endeavours to restrict its quantitative output in order, by means of all sorts of monopolistic arrangements, to prevent the price of its products from falling. In this abuse Cassel discerns the principal cause of Europe's unhappy economic state.

" If we wish to obtain a proper conception of the relation of Europe to the colonial countries," he writes, " we should do well to reflect upon a parallel case before our eyes. We have at home an industry which, broadly speaking, maintains a level of wages considerably higher than agriculture can pay, and which in consequence, as also frequently as a result of inefficient organization and management and with the help of more or less developed monopolies, keeps up the prices of its goods, whilst agriculture gets a poor price for its products. The conditions of exchange of the products of industry and of agriculture are such that they operate to the disadvantage of agriculture and to the advantage of industry. And yet industry cannot become monopolistic without being burdened with unemployed, who must be supported. The revenue from industry must therefore be divided among more than the workers, so that in the end everybody must suffer by the system."

Similar conditions prevail in most European states. Europe is therefore in the position of a trade union which has forced up wages too high and cannot therefore give full employment to all its members. Since the unemployed must be maintained, the advantage of the high prices is doubtful. Broadly speaking, it is impossible to attain a high standard of living for the population of Europe by a policy of restricted output. The remedy is to be found rather in a cutting down of costs of production and an increase in the intensity of European labour.

In Cassel's opinion, a lowering of European costs of production in industry cannot, however, be achieved by a lowering of the real standard of living of the industrial population. Cheaper industrial products and more ample imports from the colonies would, on the contrary, gradually lead to an increased real income. But at the same time the unreasonable demands of the European monopolistic industrial trade unions must be cut down and the intensity of work must be increased wherever it is now artificially restricted. Nor must we forget that there exists another, equally important, means of bringing down costs of production: more efficient organization of production and the abandonment of the policy of unnecessary restriction of output to which trusts and cartels are prone. If European labour were fully employed we should enjoy in Europe a higher standard of living than is possible under present conditions, with 10 to 20 per cent of the working population unemployed. This is one of the fundamental points in Cassel's reasoning.

It is not sufficient, however, in achieving an increased exchange of goods with transoceanic countries, that the latter should produce sufficient raw materials and that Europe should produce cheap manufactured goods. It is also necessary that the standard of living in such oversea countries should continuously rise. It is true that in the last decade, according to the Report of the League of Nations, the standard of living appears in fact to have risen in oversea countries, though by no means enough, as yet, to create such an increased consumption of European goods as is necessary for any marked improvement in the European economic position.

In real life it is not difficult to see that any raising of the standard of living of the coloured races can only be achieved by education or by the direct influence of Europeans, and that is a slow process. It is easy to adduce examples of this. Mexico is one of the richest countries on earth, but its population one of the poorest. If we take into consideration the present low level, both material and spiritual, of the Peon, we must regard a sufficient increase in his material and cultural requirements as impossible of achievement except after generations of education.

And yet Mexico is a country in which the raising of the standard of living is facilitated by great natural advantages. For this reason it is clear that one of the inevitable preliminaries to the creation of better conditions for European industry must be sought in large-scale emigration from Europe, so that the white races may introduce a new stimulus into the oversea continents, partly by the increased production and consumption which they themselves will create as settlers, and partly by the example which they will set to the natives. This can also be expressed so that a new purchasing power must be created in countries outside the European continent and Great Britain, and it is also to be observed that Russia must be considered as a country not belonging to the territory of the European economic entity.

Cassel admits that European emigration to the colonies is a necessary link in the chain of endeavour to improve Europe's position.

"A part of the European unemployed," writes Cassel, "or perhaps more correctly, a part of the youth which as it grows up constantly swells the volume of unemployment, must be sent out to the colonies, so that they may create an increased purchasing power for European products and allow more employment for those who remain at home. Europe must, he says, distribute its surplus of labour. One part must be absorbed by European industry and there busy itself in the most efficient manner in increasing to the utmost European output. The other part must emigrate to the colonies in order to increase production there. Only in this way is it possible to attain the most favourable equilibrium in the exchange of commodities between Europe and the colonies. There would seem to be no doubt that the welfare of both parts would in this way be much greater than at present."

So that even from the more optimistic point of view of Professor Cassel one arrives at the same conclusion, i.e. that nothing effective can be done to improve the economic position of Europe without carefully organized, large-scale emigration to oversea countries, in so far as such emigration constitutes the only possible reliable guarantee that the standard of living in the oversea countries will in the future be continuously raised.

This raising of the standard of living in the oversea continents must react on Europe in many ways, but especially in that the demand for European goods and the construction of roads, railways and similar undertakings in the oversea countries will be increased, as well as the demand for technical apparatus of all kinds.

It is another matter that the increased output by European industry, as assumed by Professor Cassel, must encounter numerous practical difficulties, for the execution of the plan is scarcely conceivable unless the most important customs barriers between the European states are removed and these states co-operate in the spirit which has been also so strongly emphasized by Joseph Caillaux. There is the further difficulty that the United States constitute a self-contained economic unit and that Europe, even with a considerable reduction of prices, can scarcely find a large outlet there for its goods, since the United States will resist by prohibitive tariffs every attempt to import cheap European goods.

The view has also been advanced in England that one of the reasons for the present backwardness of Europe is to be found in the fact that the European output of labour, per man per day, is less than that of the United States. This in its turn is the consequence of the highly developed organization of the trade unions, which are much more powerful in Europe than in the U.S.A. "If a worker in the United States," it is said, "makes ten articles per day and a European worker makes only six of the same kind in the same time, it is obvious that the American worker enjoys a higher standard of living than the European, and will not be willing to exchange his ten articles for six." In other words, the European worker must increase his output per hour until he reaches the level necessary to the achievement of an equally high standard of living.

It is, however, very difficult to determine whether comparisons of this sort are of any real value.

The comparisons hitherto made between American and European working output per hour or day are vitiated by the fact that conditions in the two continents are usually very different and not comparable. But from whatever point of view one regards the economic condition of Europe, and even though it may be difficult to judge matters of detail, yet there is no doubt that Europe is in a critical economic position for which there is only one conceivable remedy: different lines of economic policy in general and the organization of emigration according to a definite and far-seeing plan.

CHAPTER IV

THE OVER-POPULATION OF THE WORLD

The History of the Growth of Population

IT is a common conception that there is in the world a superfluity of food and raw materials which might comfortably support the whole of mankind, if only this natural bounty were properly distributed. But the investigations of economists have dispersed these golden dreams and have shown that the exact contrary is the case. They contend, on very good grounds, that the human race is only able to support itself under present conditions with the utmost difficulty and expenditure of energy.

In order to understand this problem it is necessary to cast a glance at the problem of the world's population. There are at the present time many times as many persons in the world as in former days. Professor Maurice Caudel affirms in an article in the " Revue Economique Internationale " that at the beginning of the Christian era there lived on the earth about 50 million beings, but in the year 1800 about 600 millions.[1]

At the present moment the population is estimated at 1,600,000,000, and it has thus multiplied threefold in 125 years. All these beings eat, and to sustain themselves they must work. Their labour presupposes increasing intensity, and the daily tension, thanks to competitors throughout the world, becomes greater and greater, while the world economy becomes more and more complicated. This result is due also to the fact that modern man is no longer satisfied with merely appeasing his hunger. He has many other demands beyond his daily bread, and the productivity which in the year 1800 sufficed to supply the modest needs of 600 million human beings would scarcely suffice nowadays, according to our author, for the same population for a week.

Professor Caudel's calculations of the population of the globe are somewhat lower than those of other writers. In the "Zeitschrift für Geopolitik," Alois Fischer recently made a comprehensive study of the world's population in historical times and at the present day.[2] To begin with, he states that

[1] Maurice Caudel: "Le rôle du facteur économique dans la politique contemporaine," "Revue Economique Internationale," pp. 216 *et seqq.* Goemaere, Bruxelles, May, 1926.

[2] Alois Fischer: "Zur Frage der Tragfähigkeit des Lebensraumes," "Z. f. Geopolitik," Heft 10, 1925, pp. 762 *et seqq.*

all statistics of population before 1800 are unreliable and the calculations very approximate. For the year 1800 he estimates a population of 775 millions. Earlier estimates are very doubtful, and for ancient times one cannot give a probable figure within some hundreds of millions. But one may venture to affirm, writes Fischer, that early developments show that broadly speaking the population tended upwards, though occasionally there was a decline in the figures. The cause of such a decline was usually war, or the consequences of war, such as epidemics and hunger, which caused greater loss of life than war itself.

Terrestrial catastrophes such as earthquakes have never occasioned so great a decline as war and epidemics. The Lisbon earthquake, which yet strongly influenced European conceptions, caused a loss of 30,000 lives. The recent earthquake in Tokio and Yokohama, on the 1st–9th September 1923, showed a casualty list of 140,000, which number, however, represents only a fifth of the annual birth surplus in Japan in recent years.

The relative increase of the human race has never been so great as in the nineteenth century and the opening years of the twentieth, when it went up as much as 1·1 per cent. That the annual increase of population became so great after 1905 was due mainly to progress in medical science, which reduced the mortality figures annually in a more rapid ratio than that of the reduction in birth figures, which began to a considerable extent about the same time.

In the year 1913 the increase in the world's population amounted to 0·9 per cent, but then came the World War, which caused great changes. In most European countries the population declined or was stationary, but whilst the population of Europe thus remained the same or was reduced, the increase of population continued, unaffected by the war, in other continents. In 1918, i.e. three and a half years after the outbreak of the war, the population outside Europe had increased, in comparison with 1914, by 26 million souls. But here too there came a set-back in the influenza epidemic of 1918, which, especially in India, reduced the world's population by about 20 million souls. In 1919 the ravages of the influenza epidemic continued. Thereupon came the famine in Russia and a further reduction of about 7 millions. The Great War was responsible for direct losses amounting to about 13 millions (about $\frac{1}{140}$ of the population of the world). In its extraordinary volume of direct mortality the World War surpassed all previous wars, in spite of the high degree of efficiency of the Red Cross service. By way of comparison it may be mentioned that the total losses in the wars of the nineteenth century amounted to about 4 millions.

If, again, one looks at the aftermath of the World War it has not, relatively speaking, had such devastating consequences as many previous wars, thanks to improved medical and hygienic conditions throughout the world.

For the first time since the war the population increased in 1920 in all the continents of the world. In Europe it increased by 2 millions and in other continents by about 5 millions. The figures have since risen somewhat higher and would appear to have become stabilized at an increase of about 0·77 per cent per annum of the total population, which is somewhat lower than before the war, when the total annual increase of population was calculated to average 16 millions, or about 0·9 per cent, of which 6 millions or 1·3 per cent belonged to Europe.

Whereas the total population of the world in 1925 was 62 millions greater than in 1924, yet Europe in 1925 had only reached the figure of 1914. In this connection it is to be noted that in Europe the distribution between the different countries has changed, and the increase in population has varied greatly in the different countries. In some countries, as for example in Soviet Russia, there has been a decrease of about 9 millions since 1914. The population has also decreased, though only slightly, in France, Poland, Austria, Lithuania, and Esthonia. Otherwise the population has everywhere increased in Europe since 1914. The population of Germany exceeds that of 1914 by 2 millions, though its capacity to feed an increasing population is much less than in 1914. Germany must therefore in one way or another dispose of its surplus population.

In Great Britain also the population has increased by 2 millions. Great Britain is moreover a country in which one can obtain a good survey of developments in the last centuries in their logical connection. It is easy to see that the increase of population has been very considerable. Great Britain was the pioneer in the industrial revolution in the nineteenth century and rejoiced in a natural prosperity hitherto unknown in the world's history, thanks to the circumstance that during the first half of the nineteenth century and as late as 1860 it could sell coal and manufactured goods in the world's market practically without competition. It thus rapidly accumulated wealth, which enabled it to maintain far more citizens than in any earlier period. In 1821 the population of England and Wales was something over 12 millions. In 1921 the number had increased to nearly 39 millions, so that the population increased threefold in a hundred years.

In Italy the population has increased since 1914 by 2 millions, and an annual addition is expected from the natural increase arising from the surplus of births over deaths of over 400,000 per annum.

In Germany, including the occupied territories, statistics show that on 1st May 1926 the number of unemployed amounted to 1,820,000, and in Great Britain during recent years the number has remained constant between 1,200,000 and 1,300,000 persons. In Great Britain the outlook is at present especially gloomy, because the prolonged coal strike has caused great losses and has further encroached on the resources of the country.

The tension on the British people has perhaps never been more acute than just in connection with the coal strike. The strike was due to the dissatisfaction of the miners with their wages and to certain technical conditions in the mines. The problem is almost insoluble, since the English coal industry, despite comparatively low wages, is carried on to a large extent at a loss, or at any rate no longer yields any considerable profit. Experts consider that at least 25 per cent of the English collieries should be closed down as they are no longer economically self-supporting. Unless coal-getting in these mines can be replaced by other, new, British mines, the number of miners must be diminished. This may happen to such an extent that a further 250,000 persons will be thrown out of work. It has been proposed that the British State should pension these workers, since some people are of opinion that this would be the cheapest way of disposing of them. This, however, would be a foolish solution. The British State already has more than enough pensioners to support in the war wounded and the ordinary unemployed. The only proper solution is to transplant these superfluous miners to another part of the world where it may be possible to procure work for them, preferably with the prospect of making them self-supporting in a near future. So long as there remain unexploited patches on the globe the economic equilibrium of the world requires that human beings should not be permitted to remain without work in areas where there is a surplus of labour, and that such surplus labour should be transferred to the place where opportunities exist for productive work. In Europe, with the exception of certain parts of France, such places do not exist. The only solution of the problem is emigration, which offers to the unemployed a new field of activity in the colonies and oversea countries.

And here we impinge once again upon the great colonial question which the governor of the German Reichsbank, Dr. Schacht, treated in an interesting address to the Deutsche Kolonialgesellschaft.[1] He affirms there with great emphasis the folly of the present distribution of the world's population on very much the same grounds as those above stated. "On the present lines of development," says Dr. Schacht, "we cannot continue. Is it reasonable that Germany should have 123 inhabitants per square kilometre when Germany's former colonies in the same area only had 4? That Belgium should have 257 inhabitants per square kilometre, but only 6 in her colonies; France 74 at home and 5

[1] Dr. Hjalmar Schacht: "Neue Kolonialpolitik," Druckerei der Reichsbank, Berlin, 1926, pp. 7 *et seqq.*

in the colonies; Portugal 65 at home and 4 in the colonies? And finally, is it reasonable that Great Britain feeds 47 millions, whilst Canada, which is more than thirty times as large, only feeds 8 millions? To put the question," says Dr. Schacht, "is to answer it." The simple and inevitable truth is that a considerable part of the population of Europe must be given the opportunity to emigrate.

A careful calculation of the increase and geographical distribution of the population of the world at the present time has been made in the above-mentioned memorandum published by the League of Nations. According to this calculation the population of the world has increased since 1913 by 5 per cent on the average, but the population of Europe, as already mentioned, by only a little over 1 per cent. But it should be noted that this low rate of increase is due, as already remarked, to the large decrease in European Russia.

The relative increase has been greatest in North and South America and around the coasts of the South Pacific, whilst the increase has been less in Asia and Africa. In spite of the low rate of increase in Europe as a whole, it appears nevertheless that certain states are greatly over-populated and suffer accordingly from severe unemployment.

If we regard the population question and the economic situation of the world from the European point of view, it is clear that European interests are opposed to those of the rest of the world. Europe cannot be reconstructed as an isolated unit, but must restore its economic balance by a common and well-thought-out policy in relation to the other continents. In an interesting essay in "The World's Work," Mr. Joseph Caillaux remarks in substance on this point: [1] There is only one remedy, not two, and that is European solidarity. People in general suppose that the only thing to be striven for is to bring back to Europe the conditions which prevailed before the Great War; but whoever is so naïve as to believe that, should look around him. There was a time, it is true, when all was easy and comfortable. The recollection of those times easily calls to mind Talleyrand's words: "Those who did not know French society before 1789, will never know how pleasant life can be." In the same way we may say that life was pleasant before 1914, so pleasant indeed that it scarcely occurred to anybody to inquire whether world conditions at that time rested on safe ground. It has since become clear that they did not, though it is no use complaining now. We must look forwards and not backwards. We must learn to understand that since all the normal laws of production, trade and credit have been upset no attempts to restore Europe can be successful until the sole remedy has been seized: that of economic accord between the various states of Europe. There were far-seeing men who

[1] "The World's Work," November 1926, pp. 35 *et seqq.*

realized this even before 1914, but they did not gain a hearing.

There are three powerful causes, in Caillaux's opinion, of Europe's troubles. The first is the unorganized and excessive production, the second the crushing burden of rates and taxes, and the third the transfer of values from one country to another. Very large sums are required, writes Caillaux, to pay the interest on international debts, and debts in themselves are so much dead weight. The living wear themselves out for the dead, or if another metaphor may be permitted, behind the producer who creates new values there stands an invisible being who steals away a larger or smaller part of them and casts it into the abyss, i.e. into the gulf of the debit accounts of the various nations.

Caillaux is therefore of the opinion that Europe's burden of international debt, especially to the U.S.A., should be considerably reduced, or completely cancelled, by common consent. He concludes his essay with these words:

> "Europe must either organize and unite or perish."

It is difficult to see how such a reduction of debt as Caillaux advocates can be achieved at present, but he is in any case right when he says that the European debt must be balanced in some way or other in relation to the rest of the world, as may be done if Europe acquires new resources in other continents, and especially if it develops new markets.

It is a pure illusion to suppose that with the help of perfected scientific work and industrial technique Europe can be reconstructed by work exclusively in the old fields of production. There is no use producing if there are no buyers. To improve the technical resources of producers and the volume of production before the economic balance between Europe and oversea countries is restored can only lead to new economic catastrophes.

Another way of escape from the dilemma must be chosen than the one-sided development of the European capacity of production. It is no longer sufficient to apply modern improved methods in the old industrial states. These methods must be transported across the oceans and must be adapted to virgin soil for the production of food-stuffs and raw materials which can be exchanged for European manufactured goods.

CHAPTER V

THE DEVELOPMENT OF JAPAN AND THE COLONIES OF THE WHITE RACES

Over-population—Japan's Colonial Policy—Industrial Development

THE alliance with England, success in the struggle against Russian expansion in the Pacific, and, finally, participation in the World War with the status of a Great Power among the victors: these are the historic events which during one generation have given to Japan its present rank. But during the years following the war Japan gained so much more, both politically and economically, that it is quite natural that she should regard herself politically and financially as the predominant power in the Pacific. In 1918 a special association was founded in Japan to safeguard Japanese interests in the Southern Pacific. It had as its special object the study of those geographical areas which it might be of importance to know in connection with the future development of the Japanese race. Ambitious plans were prepared for the purchase of land for rubber plantations and for the acquisition of iron, manganese, and coal mines, in order to procure raw materials for the Japanese steel industry.

But up to the present fate has not altogether favoured Japan's ambitions. Development was rapid during the first years after the war, industry expanded and the banks increased their turnover. But then came the above-mentioned great earthquakes in Tokio and Yokohama, which brought developments to a standstill that has even now not been overcome. Foreign countries also miscalculated this convulsion of nature in so far as they expected immense consequent purchases of raw materials. But reconstruction has not proceeded as rapidly as was anticipated, owing to lack of capital for the purpose, and great sections of the population in the affected parts of the country are suffering from poverty.

Japan lies on volcanic soil and has extensive mountain chains, so that only about 35 per cent of its area can be brought under cultivation. The available land is utilized to the utmost by intensive culture, and begins to show signs of exhaustion. In any case, it is not possible by means of more scientific culture to achieve more abundant harvests than at present.[1] The great Japanese problems

[1] This refers to the possibility of rice and grain crops, which can only be obtained in Japan in the lowlands. Of recent years plans have been prepared to utilize the mountain slopes for crops of fruit and vegetables.

remain the same as before the war, and are the consequence of the density of population which makes it impossible to feed the present population out of its own resources.[1] It is conceivable, and it has been put forward as a dream of the future for Japan, that the problem might be solved by creating a progressively increasing field of activity for the population in proportion as industry increases. Japan would then play the same part in Asia as Great Britain played in Europe by creating a large-scale industry, supplied partly by its own raw materials and partly by imports of raw materials and foodstuffs from tropical colonial possessions, so constituted that they could be easily administered and protected by the mother country. But the tropical colonies suitable for this purpose are already occupied by the white races, and nothing really of value can be obtained by Japan except by war. Moreover, industrial developments in Japan are hampered by the fact that it does not contain within its own frontiers the raw materials essential to the conduct of modern industry.

Japan lacks iron-ore, coal, and petroleum. These essential materials must therefore be imported from abroad. This circumstance explains why Japan has not only directed its attention to the tropics, but also seeks on the one hand to acquire control

[1] Cf. Helmer Key: "European Bankruptcy and Emigration," Methuen & Co., Ltd., London, 1924, pp. 38 and 41–55.

over Sachalin, and on the other hand to gain a firm footing in Manchuria and Eastern Mongolia, and to this end has endeavoured to come to an arrangement with Russia concerning China. Japan's *rapprochement* to Soviet Russia cannot be explained on any other ground than that Japan cannot give way in Manchuria, where it possesses iron-ore and coal mines, and already controls the South Manchurian railway system between Dairen and Chanychung, which has now absorbed the Korean system also. This railway system is of colossal magnitude, and has a capital of 440 million yen. Moreover, both in Manchuria and Southern Mongolia there are vast areas, suitable for agricultural colonization, which possess the advantage that climatically they are better adapted for the Japanese than are the subtropical territories.

We must remember that Japan, like Germany and Italy, requires above all things colonies suitable for the emigration of its national emigrants. Japan's so-called colonies, Korea and Formosa, are on the other hand worthless in this respect, since they are already so densely populated that they afford no room for settlers.

The importance of the colonization problem becomes manifest when one considers that the population of Japan has increased from 54,142,000 in 1914 to no less than 60,258,000 in 1923. The yearly surplus amounts to 14 per 1,000. As to Korea, the population has increased from 31st

December 1914, from 15,621,000 to 17,447,000 at the end of December 1923. The increase amounts to 13·69 per *mille*, or together about 120,000 per annum. The density of population amounted in 1923 to 79·04 per square kilometre. In Formosa conditions are similar, in so far as the population increased from 3,307,000 in December 1914 to 3,649,000 in December 1923. The annual increase per thousand inhabitants is 17·71 and the density of the population 102·29 per square kilometre.[1]

The fact that Japan lacks the possibility of peacefully acquiring suitable colonial areas has naturally evoked much bitterness against the white races among the population, and it is interesting in this connection to observe Japanese opinion on this subject. It appears that the opinion is general that the present distribution of territory is highly unjust in permitting a few nations the monopolistic use of vast territories with enormous resources, thereby compelling the remaining nations to do the best they can in restricted areas with scanty natural resources.

"Roughly speaking,"[2] writes the Japanese author Kawakami, "the land area of the earth measures 52,825,000 square miles, supporting 1,751,700,000 inhabitants.

"Of this total area the Caucasian peoples occupy or control about 46,146,084 square miles, comprising Europe,

[1] "The Twenty-fifth Financial and Economic Annual of Japan, 1925," p. 1. Cf. "Annual Report on Administration of Chosen (1922–23), Keijo," December 1924, p. 14.

[2] H. H. Kawakami: "The Real Japanese Question," New York, The Macmillan Co., 1921, pp. 231, *et seqq.*

North and South America, Australasia, and most of Africa and Asia. It will be seen that the Caucasian race, having completed the occupation of Europe and the Americas, has conquered and secured control of the whole of Australasia, almost all Africa, the greater part of Asia, as well as the adjacent islands.

" And the Caucasian peoples who control so vast a territory number only 623,000,000. In other words, there are only 13·5 Caucasians to each square mile of land.

" On the other hand, the native population of Asia number no less than 900,000,000. And yet they control only 6,679,000 square miles of territory, because Siberia and Turkestan are occupied by Russia, India by Great Britain, and Tonking and Cochin China by France, while Tibet, Chinese Turkestan, Mongolia, and Northern Manchuria, aggregating 2,655,000 square miles, are fast passing under British or Russian control. In other words, there are 134·8 Asiatics to each square mile of Asiatic land."

It is true that Asiatics are permitted to remain in India, Cochin-China, and other Asiatic territories which have come under European rule, but the fact remains that the expropriation of Asiatic territory has deprived the population of every opportunity of themselves utilizing extensive areas, with great natural resources, within their own continent.

" It cannot be disputed," Kawakami continues, " that colonies, sparsely populated yet rich in resources, are valuable assets to a nation with small, over-populated territory. They relieve the mother-country in two ways —they afford shelter to its surplus population, and they enable it to support its population at home more adequately by reason of the stimulation and increase which their products naturally offer to its commerce and industry."

The Anglo-Saxons, like some other European

nations, have laid claim to the world's richest territories, but the Asiatic peoples, who came late to market, can no longer find suitable territory for oversea colonies, and have no alternative, unless they resist, than to sacrifice their country on the altar of Western ambitions.

" Here, in a nutshell," writes Kawakami, " is a condition which should not be ignored in any consideration of international problems affecting the peoples of Asia. It is obvious that the Great Powers of the West have accumulated more land than they should rightly own—than they can hold without doing injustice to the smaller nations, which find themselves in sad plight, due to the impossibility of finding room for their surplus population. The injustice of holding such vast territories would not be so obvious if they were to recognize, in favour of the small nations, the principle of unhindered immigration and of unrestricted enterprise within those territories. It is when they erect insurmountable walls around themselves and adopt a hidebound policy of exclusion that they become a menace to the welfare of the human race.

" It seems to me that any proposition for permanent peace which fails to take into consideration the present inequitable distribution of territory, cannot be carried out without trampling upon the just claims of the smaller nations. An attempt to build permanent peace upon the *status quo* of the world seems as futile as an attempt to rear a Tower of Babel upon a foundation of sand.

" It is obvious," concludes the Japanese writer, " that a programme to establish permanent peace with justice should contain one of two propositions, namely, a more equitable distribution of territory, or the removal of the exclusive policy adopted by Western colonial Powers against Asiatic peoples."

Many of the measures referred to by the Japanese

writer which the Western Powers have introduced involve very dubious consequences. Australia, with its vast empty spaces, adopts a policy which excludes all yellow colonization, whilst at the same time the Australians only very reluctantly admit even white colonists to fill the voids. In the Far East the position is such that masses of people in the over-populated lands must gradually be forced into the empty spaces, in accordance with the irresistible law of nature that water in two connected vessels rises to the same level in order to restore equilibrium.

Since the Japanese have encountered so many difficulties in acquiring new colonies, they have sought compensation in other ways, and even before they directed their attention to China and Manchuria they experimented with "block settlements" in North America. Their great success as gardeners in California had a stimulating effect, and they endeavoured to secure a footing elsewhere on the west coast. But here too the problem has become very complicated. The United States have now completely closed their frontiers to yellow immigrants, except that the Japanese domiciled in Hawaii and possessing American citizenship have the right to settle in the U.S.A. To find a solution the Japanese have negotiated for concessions in Mexico, Chile, Peru, and other countries, but their success has for various reasons been hitherto very slight, perhaps mainly because the native population has nowhere received them favourably.

The Japanese appear to have been somewhat more successful in their colonial experiments, though only on a small scale, in the eastern states of South America. A German writer, Dr. D. Maull, considers that Japanese colonists have secured a firm footing in Brazil, and he writes that he encountered flourishing block settlements in the Sao Paolo hinterland.[1] It may be added that negotiations are at present said to be in progress for a lease of a large area of land by Brazil in the Amazon district, but of this more at a later stage. If one regards these experiments from the point of view of the white races it would appear that Japanese colonization on the east coast or the interior of eastern South America does not meet with the same objections as a mass colonization on the west coast, in so far as colonization on the eastern side of the Cordillera can scarcely be supposed to assume such proportions in relation to the remaining population as to constitute a political danger.

In the autumn of 1926 it was reported that at a trade congress in Tokio it was officially declared that Japan was about to change its colonial policy and would no longer endeavour to send emigrants to countries which did not wish to receive them. It was proposed instead to promote a so-called internal colonization, to be concentrated in the islands of Jesso and Formosa. At the same time Japan would seek to develop its industries

[1] June issue of "Geopolitik," 1926, p. 428.

and find an outlet for them in the Pacific islands.

It is difficult to know how to envisage this declaration. That Japan desires to increase its exports is an old story and a desire not at all easy to realize. As to Formosa, we have already pointed out that the island is already over-populated. The population of Jesso is, it is true, sparse, but the island does not offer a particularly attractive climate to the Japanese. One cannot avoid the suspicion therefore that the declaration is prompted more by a desire to divert general attention from Japan's need of colonies than by the existence of any well-thought-out plan for a real solution of the problem.

In spite of all the difficulties with which Japan has had to contend in recent years, the endeavour persists with undiminished energy to render the country independent of foreign countries, especially in industry. The results are not so tangible that they can as yet be statistically proved, but in the cotton industry, for example, it is easy to see that developments in Japan, as in other oversea countries, have been remarkably great. Here, indeed, is one of the industrial phenomena by which it can be shown that present developments in the world are to the disadvantage of Europe. It appears, for example, from the following table that the increase in the number of cotton spindles during the last fifteen years has been proportionally much greater in Japan and India in comparison with the correponding increase in Great Britain, Europe's largest producer.

COTTON SPINDLES (000's)[1]

	1910.	1925.
India	5,657	8,500
Japan	1,948	5,292
China	1,600	3,350
Canada	855	1,319
Brazil	1,000	1,950
Great Britain	53,397	*57,116*

It may be added that the production of raw wool and woollen goods, raw silk and silk goods is one of the departments of Japanese industry which appears to be developing rapidly.

So long as China remains powerless Japan is the Great Power of the yellow races, and it is undoubtedly Japan which will play the predominating part in the future in the event of a struggle between the white and the yellow races for supremacy over the world's resources. But such a conflict is fortunately at present not in sight. In any case, Japan has a strong will to conquer and to create for itself the place in the sun which it must claim. A peaceful solution can in that case not be found except on the assumption of such a division of colonial territory in the East as will afford sufficient room to the Japanese to procure suitable habitations for its rapidly increasing population.

Meanwhile, in considering the difficulties of Japan

[1] Sir William Clark: "Overseas Trade after the War," John Heywood, Manchester, 1920, p. 10.

one must not forget the set-back which the country suffered by the earthquake catastrophes, which, among other things, adversely affected social problems, in so far as discontent among Japanese workers, who in comparison with Europeans live under very inferior conditions, was intensified. Bolshevism has found among them a fertile soil, and the Japanese State has therefore to contend with internal political and social problems which will assuredly put the ability of its statesmen to a severe test. But with the proud traditions of Japan and with the reverence of its citizens for the State it is probable that the land of the Mikado will surmount these difficulties also.

CHAPTER VI

THE PURCHASING POWER OF THE COLONIES

A Higher Standard of Living for the Colonial Races—Collectivism the Special Form of Barbarism—The Land Question in Morocco

IN the previous chapter we have treated partly the problem of over-population and partly the changing industrial activity in many oversea countries and colonies, especially in India and Japan. Examination has shown, among other things, that the prosperity and economic independence of oversea countries has been achieved at the cost of Europe by restricting the market for European goods. But we must not suppose that this development in the new continent is all to the bad for Europe. It is clear especially that increased productivity even among the colonial races involves better wages and a consequent higher standard of life. But the *tempo* and extent of this development must be counterbalanced by other measures on the part of the white races, and above all things a great stream of emigration from Europe must be created. If these two phases of development are brought into relative equilibrium, then their inconveniences should be overcome, and a raising of the standard of living of the coloured races would be of extraordinary significance in the economic development of the world and would contribute to an improvement and expansion of the market for European goods.

The endeavour to improve the conditions of life among the coloured races is a new phenomenon. In former times Europeans treated the natives in conquered oversea countries very badly. They even went so far as practically to exterminate the native population, or to subject it to a more or less complete slavery, as usually happened in the Spanish colonial empire. The great pioneers of the modern conception of the colonial problem were Wilmot Horton and Edward Gibbon Wakefield,[1] the creators of England's colonial policy at the beginning of the nineteenth century, though one should not forget the well-known Swedish philanthropist Carl Bernhard Wadström (1746–99). The latter, who made a voyage of exploration to Africa at the expense of Gustavus III, lived for the most part abroad, at first in London and then in Paris. His efforts were directed to the foundation of colonial enterprises, and above all he laboured

[1] Helmer Key: "European Bankruptcy and Emigration," Methuen & Co., Ltd., London, 1924. See pp. 54 *et seqq.*

zealously for the abolition of slavery. In many respects he was far before his time, and was one of the few who realized the necessity of procuring markets across the ocean for European manufactured goods. What is remarkable is that he not only envisaged white colonization, but also laboured for the education of the coloured races. He remarks that hitherto the Europeans had principally encouraged the natives to buy powder and gin, but that they ought instead to endeavour to awaken their interest in other and more useful articles. In order to achieve this purpose it was necessary to awaken their intellectual interests, or to familiarize them with a certain amount of luxury.

"Mere animal instinct impels," writes Wadström,[1] "uncivilized tribes to procure mere necessaries: wishes for innocent gratifications would stimulate them to cultivation, which would furnish equivalents for the objects of their new desires. And when they are once brought to bestir themselves, and are reconciled to regular, but moderate, labour, the improvement of their understanding will follow of course. For a people who have acquired habits of application, and whose industry, having secured them from want, affords them leisure for thought, will not be long without a desire for moral and intellectual improvement: or, at least, many individuals will feel, and hasten to gratify, this desire, and will gradually impart a degree of knowledge and refinement to the whole community."

In olden times Europeans practised beyond the seas only a robber policy. Colonists sought only

[1] C. B. Wadström: "An Essay on Colonization." London. 2 vol., 1794–95. Cf. Vol. 2, ch. 3, "Civilization in General," pp. 18–24.

gold and raw materials and afterwards space to be settled by new-comers. How the native population fared was a matter of indifference except in so far as labour was required. Conditions in the colonies are now improved in this respect. Room for white immigrants is still sought, but the natives are treated better. Regard is had not only to the white man's interests, but the development of the colonial native races is also fostered. The aim of colonization is no longer restricted to the promotion of exports of raw materials and foodstuffs to the mother country. A local culture is envisaged by raising the standard of living of the native population. This can be achieved in the main only by the development of tillage and live-stock farming. The coloured races usually lead a nomadic life and move with their herds from one pasturage to another. The idea of property is little developed, and even when these races settle down to a primitive sort of tillage the usual form of property is that of collective village ownership. For this purpose the race is divided up into a number of small tribes, each of which leads an independent life, and each is subject to a chief. The individual member of the tribe has no interest in the work he performs and submits to it only under compulsion. Not a little of the apathy, idleness and backwardness of the coloured races may be attributed to the absence of all individual stimulus to work.

These primitive collective institutions of property

exist, or did exist originally, everywhere outside the European continent, and conditions are exactly the same whether one considers present-day Africa, the South Pacific Islands, or Latin America at the time when it was discovered by the Spaniards. Property is collective and it may be established as a fact which our European Socialists and Communists might well remember—that ethnographically collectivism is the special form of property of barbarism.

Among the coloured races there exist very varied potentialities of development, but in one respect they are identical: there is only one means of developing a higher civilization among them, and that is to instruct them in practical agriculture and to settle them. The peculiar collectivist institutions must be abolished and instead of property being the property of the village, the family, or the tribe, a new individualistic form of property must be created which will transform the nomad into a settled, preferably land-owning, peasant.

The development of civilization is the result of a transition from communism to individualism, or, if the phrase be preferred, to Western economy. The effects of this change of system have been described by many recent writers on colonial problems, and all emphasize strongly the advantage of allowing the natives to cultivate their own soil, and of giving them the right to sell their goods direct and freely to the purchaser, so that they may have the opportunity to obtain the highest market price, which in its turn must act as a natural spur to increased effort.[1]

By this we do not mean to suggest that it would be generally possible to introduce among the coloured races of the colonies a division of the land of the same character as European small holdings. Experience has shown, on the contrary, that tropical undertakings must, as a rule, be conducted in the form of large plantations, but this does not exclude the possibility, even in such cases, of numerous opportunities for individual activity on the part of the native.

Numerous large combinations for agriculture and industry have been organized by Europeans in the tropics, which have approached a rational solution of the problem of educating the native. The most important thing is to raise the native to a standard of comfort which may constitute a foundation for further development. It is not possible to begin by instilling into natural man any sort of higher ideals or civilized interests. The essential thing here is always the purely material—which is also the experience of missionaries.

The transition from collective to individual ownership usually encounters very great resistance, and

[1] See, for example, Hugh Edward Egerton: "British Colonial Policy in the Twentieth Century," Methuen, London, 1922, p. 196 and elsewhere. Also L. C. A. Knowles: "The Economic Development of the British Overseas Empire," George Routledge & Sons, Ltd., London, 1924, p. 163 and elsewhere.

as a typical example of how complex the problem can be we may cite the developments during the last decade in French Morocco.

In the beginning all land in Morocco belonged to the original inhabitants, the Berbers. These were a restless nomadic people inhabiting the mountainous districts, from which they drove their flocks from one pasturage to another. Every tribe had its own special territory. The partition of the pasturages within these territories was determined in each tribe by a sort of council of elders, called the "djemâa." The boundaries of the various tribal pasturages were vague, and not infrequently there arose bloody feuds between the tribes for the best bits. The Arabs conquered the country, but they never succeeded in completely imposing their own system of ownership. The Berbers withdrew into the mountains and succeeded by stiff passive resistance in maintaining their demand for a collective system. Some districts, it is true, were appropriated by the Sultan, but no clear principles of the law of property were ever laid down. The result was that the systems of ownership of the various peoples were very much confused.

Sometimes it happened, for example, that the Berbers, who mostly lived in the mountains, descended into the plains, intermarried with the Arabs, abandoned their nomadic life, and began to till the soil. In such cases the Berbers maintained their own institutions of property, in spite of the Arabs, and the Berber who cultivated the soil was regarded as its owner.

When the French came to Morocco they found four different institutions of property. Firstly, private possessions which could be bought and sold. Such possessions were, however, few, and were restricted for the most part to real property in the towns. Secondly, beyond comparison the greatest area of the land, consisting of the collectively owned Berber land, controlled by the "djemâa" of the various tribes. Thirdly, the "maghzen" or private possessions of the Sultanate; and fourthly, certain properties administered by pious Mussulman foundations.

It may be added that by ancient custom the "djemâa" had not the right to sell land, though they might lease agricultural land for a maximum period of ten years. When European settlers wished to acquire land this leasehold system gave rise to great abuse. The French had no idea of the native Moroccan system of property. Leases held by Arabs were sold to Europeans as if they conferred real titles to the soil, and Europeans, who were not aware that they were only valid for ten years, sought to acquire the oldest titles possible; in other words, the less valuable the title, the more they paid. The result was an incredible confusion, for which the Sultan had to bear the blame. The consular offices of the European Powers made earnest representations, but all that could be established was that the good Moroccans had cheated Europeans by selling land which did not belong to them.

In order to introduce some sort of order into the system the French had to go back to the period before the Arab conquest and restore the collective ownership of all land under the " djemâa," in order to evolve from it a new system of ownership. This reversion was necessary because there was no other starting-point, since no free land, even including that belonging to the Moroccan State, existed any longer. This was due also to the circumstance that the Sultan Mouley Hafid had, before his abdication in 1912, frittered away almost the whole of the State possessions by donations or otherwise. In this case too a troublesome and comprehensive reconstruction had to be effected.

There is now perfect order and the conditions of ownership have been determined on definite principles. That this has been done is the lasting merit of the former Governor-General of Morocco, Marshal Lyautey. The collective ownership of the Berbers was legally confirmed in 1916, but at the same time the powers of the " djemâa " were restricted and their administration of property was placed under the control of a specially appointed council in which there sat representatives of the French Colonial Office, the Sultanate and the " djemâa." The function of this Council was to superintend the activity of the " djemâa," and it should be noted that the right was conferred on the " djemâa," in case all its members desired the division of a property, to distribute it among the chiefs of the tribe with the bestowal of rights of personal ownership. Such resolutions must be submitted to the council for approval.

The various tribes can no longer change pasturages, but have become permanently settled to the extent that definite districts have been allotted to them. In this manner it has been sought to avoid all future disputes among them as to pasturages and cultivated land. In connection with this division of the land among the various Berber tribes, large districts were released which formerly belonged to the Berbers and were at the same time transferred to the State, which was commissioned to split them up and sell them to intending colonists. The "djemâa" cannot itself directly sell land, but if it wishes to sell a larger or smaller part of its collective land, it must first transfer this land to the State, which is thus always an intermediary in the breaking up, or sale, of small parcels. By confirming the Berbers as permanent settlers within limited districts, and by the regulations introduced concerning the breaking up or cession of the collective lands Marshal Lyautey created the security for a complete, though gradual, transition from collective to individual rights of property, and thereby rendered possible modern management and European enterprise in Morocco.

Difficulties similar to those experienced by France

in Morocco have also been encountered by Europeans in all the African colonies, and the history of British colonization in Africa shows how various methods have been experimentally adopted in order to solve the problem of property rights and to stimulate the natives to work. In India this problem has not offered such great difficulties, but on the other hand there has been no less difficulty in establishing a system of law which would satisfy European ideas. Collective agriculture exists, or has existed, in all countries. The Russian " mir " persisted in a form of collective ownership right down to the last revolution. In the rest of Europe, including Sweden, collective agriculture has never been fully established. There, individual ownership has existed side by side with village communities since the earliest times, which later form of ownership gradually decreased in extent, and during the course of the nineteenth century disappeared almost entirely. But the most interesting and most complete forms of state or communalistic ownership occurred in America before Columbus. In its most pronounced form the collective system appears to have prevailed in Peru during the Inca period, but also under the old Aztec *régime* in Mexico agriculture was very largely based on similar principles of property. As the Mexican land question was the cause of the recent revolutions in Mexico, and is to some extent involved in the present conflict between Church and State, I shall endeavour in the next chapter to survey the development of the land question in Mexico from the earliest to the most modern times, whilst indicating the general foundation of the modern Mexican agrarian policy.

CHAPTER VII

THE LAND QUESTION IN MEXICO

Early American Collectivism—Agrarian Policy and Revolutions

WHEN we speak of a Mexican estate we think primarily of the well-known hacienda of the Indian tales of our boyhood, by which we understand an estate of great extent and on the whole self-supporting. The proprietor of a hacienda (hacendado) is a type of landowner whom the visitor to Mexico often meets. Many of these haciendas are of immense extent. There are some with an area of as much as 250,000 acres. Only rarely is a hacienda less than 2,500 acres. In order to facilitate the management of these huge estates they are usually subdivided into smaller lots, so-called ranchos, each under its own major-domo. Some ranchos, however, are not altogether self-supporting. The word "rancho" would appear originally to have signified primarily a cattle ranch.[1]

[1] Regarding the Mexican agrarian question, see especially George McCutchen McBride: "The Land Systems of Mexico," American Geographical Society, New York, 1923.

It is to be noted in this connection that cattle ranches did not exist in Aztec Mexico, which entirely lacked domestic animals. One of the first practical measures of the Spanish "conquistadores" was therefore the provision of large imports from Spain of horses, mules, oxen, cows, sheep, and goats. The plough, drawn by oxen and mules, replaced the spade of the Indians and rendered possible a more intensive culture of the soil. Instead of human beings horses and mules or ox-drawn wagons were used for transport, which was thus very much improved.

The labourers on a hacienda are partly Indians and partly Mestizos, a race of half-bloods arising from the crossing of Spaniard and Indian, and commonly called peons. They have now abandoned their national costume to a large extent and have forgotten their original language. The pure Indians are to be found mostly in districts where, even at the time of the Spanish invasion, an agricultural population existed, living in villages, which could easily be enslaved. Such conditions prevailed especially in the Mesa Central and Yucatan. In other parts of the country, especially in the arid plains of the north, there was in Cortes' time no settled population, and the present population consists in the main of white settlers.

The peon has lived for many generations on the estate on which he is employed, and to which he is tied by strong economic bonds, as he is in such heavy debt to the proprietor for advances that he cannot repay. It has therefore always been difficult for him to free himself. By an amendment to the constitution of 1917 it is provided that the peon shall be paid in cash, and not as formerly by means of chits valid as a settlement at the hacienda stores. Besides the haciendas there have existed in Mexico since time immemorial estates owned by Indian villages, collectively administered, which are now commonly known by the name of "ejidos" (Latin *exitus*). This form of property was an important foundation of the system of property in olden Mexico. It has even been maintained that no other form of land ownership or leasehold was known; that the administration was entirely democratic; and that the estates of the privileged classes were only the land of such village communities which private individuals had received as a concession, with a right to the usufruct. It is also possible that such was in fact the case in a very remote antiquity, but it is equally certain that long before the conquest of Cortes great changes had been effected which destroyed the equality of land division, so that a new form of leasehold and freehold was created, closely resembling modern forms of ownership. Especially there existed village land which had been ceded to private families, who retained the peons as slave leaseholders, bound to the soil.

It can be established that in Montezuma's time there existed side by side with collective agriculture a landed aristocracy and a land system which may very well be characterized as feudal. This latter system developed to an enormous extent during the Spanish supremacy by continuous partitions into fiefs or otherwise, to the great detriment and eventual complete suppression of the independent small-holders, and also to the disadvantage of the collective administration of the villages.

The Spaniards accomplished by the conquest of Mexico a triple object: firstly, the expansion of the Spanish empire; secondly, the spread of the Christian religion; and thirdly, the acquisition of wealth. To achieve the last purpose the Spaniards had recourse to the system of grants, called "encomiendas" or "repartimientos." The process consisted in dividing up a certain number of groups of Indians in a sort of vassalage under Spanish officers or their subordinates. Every such Spanish governor ruled over one or more Indian chief and his subordinates, who was responsible for the cultivation of the land, for work in the mines, and for transport for the governor (encomendero). The governor was hereby granted a village or group of villages, which constituted his encomienda. The numerous towns and villages of the old Aztec kingdom were rapidly divided up among the conquerors, whereupon the governors seized the opportunity of themselves collecting the taxes. The system of grants was introduced to enable the Spaniards to profit by the work of the Indians and to develop the resources of the country, but it was not long before the system lost its original character. The Spanish governors soon became accustomed to regard the districts granted to them as their personal property, and the native Indians as their slaves. As an example of these great transfers of land in earlier times may be mentioned the grants to Cortes, to the Duke of Atrisco, and to Joan Jaramillo, whom Cortes married off to his celebrated Indian mistress and helpmeet, the beautiful Marina.

Originally it was prescribed that possession of the encomiendas could be withdrawn by the King at any time, but gradually conditions changed so that the grants could be inherited through one or more generations, until finally in 1629 this right of inheritance was extended to the fifth generation, whereby possession was for practical purposes permanently vested in the family. Many haciendas have also arisen in a different manner, as when they simply developed from estates previously held by Aztec chiefs but were attached as legitimate booty, after the conquest, by the Spanish soldiery.

In many cases land was also given to Spanish warriors as a reward for services: to the infantry, so-called "peonias," and to the cavalry, so-called "caballerias." If the soil was satisfactorily occupied and cultivated for four years the holder became entitled to full ownership. By intermarriage with Indian women these small Spanish landowners soon became mixed up with the native population and gave rise to the now so populous race known as the mestizos. This group of landowners is all the more interesting as it affords the only example of Spaniards becoming real colonists.

Another method of forming large estates arose during the colonial period by the acquisition of land by ecclesiastical bodies. According to Spanish law churches and monastries could not, it is true, own land, but the King of Spain could issue special licences, and already in Cortes' time donations of real property were made to religious institutions. Even in the middle of the eighteenth century the accumulation of land in a few hands was favoured, but then arose the question of the partition of the largest estates, especially in connection with the resolution to confiscate the Jesuit estates. In 1767 the Jesuits were expelled from Spanish territory. The Jesuits possessed in Mexico a large number of haciendas, including the most productive in the country. These estates were confiscated and placed under the administration of the Direción General de Temporalidades. Of these estates 128 were offered for public sale, but owing to religious opposition the realization was only slow, and even at the end of the colonial period, in 1810, many of these estates were still unsold and were administered by the Real Hacienda, i.e. by the Royal Treasury.

Reliable information as to the extent of the

Church estates in earlier times is lacking. After the War of Independence it was calculated that about half of the land in the country belonged to the Catholic Church.

During the first half of the nineteenth century there arose a violent agitation, which gave rise to several civil wars, for confiscation of Church property. Many estates were sequestrated, but a considerable number remained in possession of the Church. Complete sequestration of all Church estates was resolved upon by the national congress of 1856 and confirmed by the new constitution in 1857. Conditions were made even more stringent by a decree of President Benito Juarez, which provided that all ecclesiastical property must be nationalized. This was pure confiscation and there was no question, as formerly, of compensation. All this led to great confusion, and no real order was restored until 1892, when the conservative administration of Diaz confirmed the titles of all holders of nationalized land and the reform again came to naught.

The present conflict between Church and State in Mexico, which President Calles calls "political measures for enforcing the laws of Mexico," affords in fact nothing new, but is merely an adaptation of the constitution of 1917. The demand that episcopal palaces, churches, schools, convents, and other buildings used for religious purposes, should be nationalized is not in accord with the law of 1857, but is based on the more stringent provisions of the law of 1917. As in the action begun by Juarez against the Church, so also now there is no intention of paying any compensation whatever. It is a question of pure confiscation.

The sequestration of Church property is still a great economic problem. President Calles offers some interesting information on this point in an article in "Foreign Affairs." [1] According to him Mexican citizens possess only one-third of the Mexican national wealth. The remainder is held by foreigners. But of this third about 60 per cent, of an estimated value of over 1,500 million pesos, is said to belong directly or indirectly to the Church, It is natural, therefore, that the head of the State should be anxious to attach this immense wealth.

Of great importance also is the present conflict over the hacienda system and the endeavour to create a stable population of small-holders.

It appears from what has been said that there exist in Mexico both individual and collective systems of property, and that these two systems have now existed irreconcilably side by side for centuries, so that on the one hand the privately owned estates have grown to unreasonable proportions, and on the other hand the collective tillage has prevented the development of modern agriculture, based on private ownership. The result of this development has been that of the

[1] "Foreign Affairs," New York, October 1926, Vol. 5, No. 1, p. 2.

rural population only a very small proportion tills its own soil. A few rich landowners rule the land, and the remaining rural population has lived, and still lives, in very narrow and straitened conditions. The most important agrarian states are situated in the Mesa Central, i.e. Mexico, Michoacan, and Aguas Calientes. In the state of Mexico[1] the rural population comprises about 84 per cent of the total. If one includes communal soil, there are over 100,000 heads of families who are landless, as against 850 private owners. The situation is the same in Michoacan. The rural population there amounts to about 830,000, or about 84 per cent of the total population. The division of the land is here somewhat better, with about 100,000 landless heads of families, against 4,518 landowners, including communal owners. In Aguas Calientes there are 14,000 heads of families, of whom only 505 occupy their own land. In the states east and west of the central plateau conditions are similar. Thus, for example, in Morelos there are 140 landowners out of 28,000 inhabitants. In Oaxaca and Vera Cruz the situation is analogous, some hundred thousand land-

[1] Mexico is a federal republic, i.e. a republic which, on the model of the U.S.A., consists of an association of federated states, each with its governor and parliament, but all subject to a Federal President, Government and Parliament, which has its seat in a special Federal District, which consists of the City of Mexico and its immediate neighbourhood. The State of Mexico constitutes an area distinct from the Federal District.

less heads of families and some hundred, at best some thousand, owners. In the northern states on the West Coast, such as Sinaloa, the conditions are the same, i.e. a rural population of 56,000 heads of families, in round numbers, of whom 53,000 are landless.

What has been said should suffice to show that an even distribution of the land is lacking in all the Mexican states, either in the fruitful areas in the Mesa Central, the damp tropical districts in the gulf, the arid western coast districts, or the torrid, desert-like plains of the north. Everywhere one finds the same accumulation of land in a few hands, a minute number of small-holders and an uncertain and fluctuating number of part-owners of communal land. In all the states the percentage of landless inhabitants is very high, and it is evident that historical developments have favoured the growth of a latifundian system such as exists in a similar form in all Spanish-American countries. It is calculated that in the middle of the nineteenth century about 5 millions of the rural population were landless. It is also considered that at the end of Diaz's Government the number of cultivators who did not own their land was more numerous than ever before in Mexican history. This circumstance also contributed more than anything else to the downfall of Diaz. A Mexican historian, Señor Molina Enriques,[1] writes :

[1] Molina Enriques : " Los grandes problemas nacionales," Mexico City, 1909, p. 124.

"We would also point out that the French Revolution sequestrated not only Church land but also that of the nobility, and it is just that which must of necessity be done in Mexico either now, as we would wish, by peaceful means, or else by a revolution, which must come sooner or later."

The necessity for agrarian reform constituted the principal motive of Madero's revolution against Diaz. Other slogans were also raised, such as an effective general suffrage and no right of re-election of the president after a four-years term of office. But this is not a programme especially attractive to the peon. The slogan "The land for the people" had, on the other hand, a great effect. Even illiterate persons had a conception of what that meant. The landless person knew that even two generations back his ancestors had owned their own land, or had been part owners in the ejidos which had subsequently been partitioned. The hope of recovering their lands filled many hearts with a simple enthusiasm. It was therefore easy to enlist landless peons as soldiers by holding out the prospect to them of a partition of the land, or at any rate by the hope of obtaining rich booty by plunder.

But when the land was sequestrated during the revolution no consistent plan was followed. It was sought to sequestrate, and to split up into small holdings, land which had been leased to companies or private persons whenever the original grant was considered to be contrary to the law. According to official reports about 15 million hectares reverted to the State at the end of 1918. Some of these estates have been partitioned, others have been placed under the administration of the various states in anticipation of subsequent partition. Not a few are in the hands of military adventurers, who have profited by the civil war. The misfortune is that the reform at which the revolution rightly aimed gave rise to numerous abuses and seizures. Thus, for example, a report to the "Corporation of Foreign Bondholders" states that the adoption of the new land laws has occasioned great difficulties.[1]

"Agriculture in Mexico has," it is stated, "in the opinion of most people, suffered as a result of the agrarian law of 1920, which had the laudable object of breaking up large, unwieldy estates to provide lands for the working element, with a view towards the encouragement of cultivation. Unfortunately, however, according to the reports received, the land-commissioners have not confined themselves to expropriating fallow lands, but have often chosen good lands in full cultivation, frequently with ripening crops. They are even reported to have taken in some cases land worked by tenant farmers, which they had rented in a virgin state and cultivated for years.

"The result has been the restriction of cultivation and the promotion of discord and difficulties between landed interests, natives, and the Government."

The sequestration of these large estates was not, however, the main thing. As a result of the inability of the peons to take care of themselves and occupy their own land the Mexican Government could find

[1] "Fiftieth Annual Report of the Council of the Corporation of Foreign Bondholders for the year 1923," Council House, 17, Moorgate, London, p. 259.

no other solution than to endeavour by a series of laws to restore the ejidos to the villages which had formerly owned them.[1]

Many towns and villages have recovered their ejidos under this law, and reports received show that the sequestrations have proceeded in fairly good order. In the City of Mexico a Comisión Nacional Agraria was established for the whole of Mexico, which co-operates with similar institutions in the other Mexican states. Opinions on the new legislation still vary:

> "This sort of legislation," writes Mr. Chisholm,[2] "if generally adopted throughout the Republic, will certainly solve one aspect of the agrarian problem in that it will put the peon on the land. It is another question, though, whether the peon will succeed in increasing, or even maintaining, production from the soil on his own proprietorship. However, the Department of Agriculture is being organized to assist the small farmer in every possible way to cultivate the soil intelligently by means of agricultural colleges, experimental stations, paid travelling instructors, and subsidized agricultural societies, in the schools and villages."

Chisholm had himself inspected agricultural schools and sample exhibitions in the neighbourhood of Mexico, and found them well organized in comparison with similar institutions in Canada.

[1] The following laws bear upon this subject: Carranza's decree of 6th January 1915, Par. 27, in the new Mexican Constitution of 1917, the law on ejidos of the 28th December 1920, and the Reglamento Agrario of 10th April 1922.

[2] Major H. A. Chisholm, M.C., Canadian Trade Commissioner to Cuba: "Mexico as a Field for Exports," Ottawa, Thomas Mulvey, 1921, p. 12.

Both instructors and students did excellent work and showed great enthusiasm for the future agricultural development of Mexico. The Federal Council had also instituted a special department for the purchase of modern agricultural machinery with the object of re-selling to small-holders on convenient terms of payment and for interest-free loans. The department had been, so far as Mr. Chisholm could judge, quite successful, and a number of machines had been sold, although in many districts the use of modern implements is still very restricted, owing to the cheapness of labour. Tractors especially were found to be too costly to introduce.

It is hard to say whether this opinion is capable of general application. In any case, it is probable that the results in districts directly under the control of the Federal Government are vastly superior to those achieved in the remoter parts of the country. A foreign diplomat accredited to Stockholm, who had lived in Mexico during Carranza's presidency, related to the writer that he had seen some very curious instances of unsuccessful attempts to partition the land among Indian small-holders.

" A large landowner of my acquaintance," he said, " who had his estates in the vicinity of Mexico City, made an experimental partition of his land among the small-holders on his estate. There was great rejoicing. The population arranged a ' fiesta ' in Mexican fashion, with refreshments, dancing, music, and fireworks, but when pay-day arrived all the new small-holders went to their former employer and asked for their weekly wages. He explained that they could no longer have any wages as they were entitled to retain the product of the soil. But this they had not understood. They prayed him to take back his land, which they did not want. They preferred to have their former wages and to be released from their new owners' rights, which they did not understand how to use."

A very curious episode arising from the Mexican land sequestration is afforded by the confiscation of Mrs. Rosalie Caden Evans's hacienda San Pedro Coxtocan, situated in the Puebla valley, which at the time caused a great stir in the world's Press. The case is also a striking example of the dishonest propaganda which interested correspondents disseminate from Mexico so soon as anything occurs which may be characterized as injurious to Mexico, and of the manner in which everything is grossly exaggerated.

Mrs. Evans appears to have been a gifted but extremely eccentric lady of American origin, married to an Englishman resident in Mexico, Mr. Harry Evans. The estate in question was an old Spanish hacienda which had fallen into decay, but which the Evans pair had acquired by ordinary purchase. By hard work and financial sacrifice they had raised the property to a high pitch of prosperity. Mr. Evans died in November 1917, and Mrs. Evans herself assumed the management of the hacienda. In the Press telegrams it was reported that the Mexican Government wished to expropriate Mrs. Evans and that she defended herself. Diplomatic relations with Great Britain were broken off. But Great Britain's *chargé des archives* in Mexico, Mr. H. H. C. Cummins, who on his own initiative posed as a kind of self-appointed diplomatic representative of his country, and who signed himself "His Britannic Majesty's Representative," took it upon himself to assist her and intervened with representations on the subject to various persons. If one reads the British White Paper on the incident which was subsequently published, one derives from it a surprising conception of the whole incident, which, if it had not had such a painful termination, would have primarily produced only an impression of comedy.[1]

The San Pedro Coxtocan hacienda comprises an area of 2,700 acres, but the part which the national agrarian commission wished to expropriate, against compensation in bonds, or by a later concession against cash, did not consist of more than 200 hectares. The telegrams to the foreign Press were such as to create the impression that the whole estate had been expropriated.

It is stated in one passage of Mr. Cummins's letter that a part of the irrigation plant was situated on the expropriated portion, but it does not appear clear from the context whether this fact would cause any injury to the rest of the estate or would give rise to any abuse. The expropriation was to

[1] Daisy Caden Petters: "The Rosalie Evans Letters from Mexico," The Bobs Merrill Co., Indianapolis, 1926.

be made in accordance with the provision of the law on ejidos of 1920. It referred to the transfer of the portion in question to the village of San Matteo Capultitlan, Hoejotzingo, which village was considered to have a claim to it as being old ejido land. Mrs. Evans, however, would under no circumstances forgo the least part of the land which she considered she had honestly acquired, and resorted to armed resistance.

In the earlier days of the revolution the hacienda of Mrs. Evans had been partially burnt down and plundered by the Mexican mob, and the Federal Government, in order to protect her life and property, had stationed troops on the hacienda. Naturally these troops had received no orders to assist Mrs. Evans in her resistance to the land surveyors and the local police during the process of expropriation.

A somewhat curious impression is made by a report by Mr. Cummins of 21st May 1924 to the then Prime Minister, Mr. J. Ramsay MacDonald, in which he relates how he, together with the Mexican lieutenant, witnessed, as distant spectators, how Mrs. Evans, mounted on horseback and escorted by two Federal soldiers whom she had persuaded to accompany her, with a revolver in her hand compelled the expropriation officers to withdraw. Mr. Cummins certainly did advise Mrs. Evans not to resist any longer the representatives of the law, but it is impossible to escape the impression that the negotiations were conducted with very little diplomacy and tact, and it appears certain that Mr. Cummins might have prevented the unfortunate issue if he had displayed greater self-control and had been possessed of more experience.

After some time Mrs. Evans applied to the Federal Government for the withdrawal of the military guard, as all was then quiet. This request was granted and she was left, by her own action, unprotected. Soon afterwards she was surprised in the road whilst riding, and was shot from behind. It may be added that Mr. Cummins offended the Mexican Government by the assertion in one of his reports that the hacienda had been burnt and plundered by the Mexican Federal troops, which was naturally regarded as an insult to the Mexican army and which compelled the Mexican Government to expel Mr. Cummins from the country. The statement is the more curious, because in another report Mr. Cummins relates that the hacienda was burned and plundered, not by the soldiery, but by an armed mob.

It is evident that with an agricultural population at so low a stage of development as that of the Indian peon there must be great difficulties in introducing the small-holding system, since the peons are quite incapable of improving the soil by their own efforts. Attempts to introduce such a law may therefore have quite different consequences from those intended, and it is to be feared that the results will be the same as those which followed Juarez's attempted reform in the 'fifties, i.e. that the Indian small-holder will sell his newly-acquired land and thereby become freed from the soil. He will then strike out for himself and seek work as a day-worker in the mines, factories, or on the railways. A flight from the land would then occur and a floating population would arise as a menace to public order and security. Many would leave the land for the towns, where they would form a new proletariat. And that is not all. Experience has shown already that there would be an emigration from Mexico. And this emigration would not be merely a question, as formerly, of seasonal employment in Texas, Arizona, and California, or other neighbouring states of the U.S.A., but the peons would emigrate never to return. It must be remembered that the U.S.A. immigration restrictions do not apply to the neighbouring states. The peon has therefore free entry, and it is in the same manner that many Japanese and Chinese have been smuggled into the United States, and especially into California. The problem is all the more acute as just in the southern states of the U.S.A. there is a great shortage of labour, due to the fact that since the war the negroes have moved north. The tendency is therefore to replace these negroes by Mexican Indians, which is by no means to the advantage of Mexico. The peons also emigrate to the Central American republics, such as Guatemala, where the economic development is at present very rapid, in order to find regular employment. The situation in Mexico is rendered even worse by professional politicians and social reformers whose unripe modern ideas the peons do not understand. In any case the land question is far from solved, and it is still by no means certain that present reforming efforts will be more successful than earlier ones.

Mexican land reform is not restricted, as I have already said, to the ejidos. More comprehensive sequestrations have also been attempted. Special states, such as Michoacan, Zacatecas, and Yucatan, have passed laws with the object of partitioning haciendas into small lots. But in this case no attempts have been made to reintroduce communal ownership, the sole object having been to divide up the large estates. Nor has there been pure confiscation, for the State has been willing to pay a certain purchase price. In Michoacan, for example, this has been fixed at an amount corresponding to the assessment value plus 10 per cent and the value of improvements. Bonds are offered in payment payable in twenty annual payments. It is not yet clear how far this legislation has succeeded, but in one state at least the laws have been repealed as impracticable.

The Federal Congress in Mexico has also endeavoured to introduce a general agrarian law for all the federated states. This reform aims at a change in the leasehold system. All payment by personal service is to be abolished, and instead of it a certain rate of interest or tax in cash is to be introduced. All the larger estates, haciendas and ranches would not be expropriated: exceptions would be those estates which are managed as industrial units or are technically well equipped. Many of the latter belong to companies. Thus, for example, there is in the Californian peninsula an American cattle-breeding company which owns about 3 million acres. In some states, where a division of the land is not necessary, as for example in Colima, there is no question of expropriation. There are also many large landowners who properly develop the resources of the land, or at least try to do so. In principle the object to be aimed at is not to resort to expropriation wherever an estate is properly managed.

The general conclusion is that the Mexican land laws hitherto adopted or proposed are by no means so revolutionary in character as is generally supposed in Europe. These laws are not the expression of any Bolshevist or communistic ideas in the European sense of the words, but have their foundation in the historical development of Mexico. The land reform problem has been acute since the time of the Aztecs, i.e. since long before Cortes. Neither is the purpose of the reforms to abolish the large estates, but only to reduce their size in order at their expense to foster small holdings. Neither is it proposed to reintroduce communal ownership in the form of ejidos, except as a form of transition to private ownership in proportion as the peons are educated to independent activity. But the great question is how to effect this education. It is difficult for a sceptic to understand how this can be achieved unless Mexico resolves to promote considerable and well-organized immigration, especially from Europe, not only to replace the now emigrating peons, but also to retain them and to educate them. Model farms should be established which might serve as an example to the peons, though probably it is not sufficient to engage European experts for this purpose. Transfers of not inconsiderable estates must be conceded to European settlements. Especially German agriculturists and experts—the more so as Germans are highly esteemed in Mexico—would be of great value in this case. But a necessary condition must be that the Mexicans make up their minds to land concessions without any irritating restrictions. At present the outlook in this respect is dark, in so far as the Federal Government is contemplating a colonization law which, among other things, will prescribe that the foreign colonist must mix with the Mexican. The Government declares that it hopes in this way to prevent the development within the republic of exclusively foreign block settlements. It wishes to avoid such a development as occurred in Brazil among the German colonists. Experience has shown, however, that the foreign colonization of Mexico can only succeed where foreigners concentrate in special localities, to the exclusion of the natives. In other words, it seems to be necessary to form colonies consisting exclusively of foreign colonists. Such colonies must of course have the right subsequently to employ Mexican labour in order to train it. As a later development Mexican block settlements could be formed, or existing Mexican agricultural communities might be reorganized with the assistance of foreign experts.

Historically it is clear that the latifundian system, with peon slaves bound to the soil, is an antiquated agricultural system, but one should not on that account push the demand for small-holdings too far. The size of the estates must vary according to geographical and climatic conditions. In many places the large estates must be retained, but in others it is surely possible to introduce small-holdings in the modern sense.

Economic, social and political considerations require a reduction in the size of the haciendas and an increase in the number of ranchos and small-holdings. But the success of the projected legislation is entirely a question of education. If the programme of Mexican reform can be carried through, a great work will have been done and the foundation will have been laid for further developments, but whether it will succeed, the future alone can show.

Despite the fact that in relation to its development only a comparatively small area of Mexican soil is cultivated, yet it may be assumed that the advance of Mexican agriculture will be of immense significance to the rest of the world. It has been estimated that the yield amounts to only about 50 per cent of what it was 125 years ago, which clearly shows the backward state of Mexican agriculture. Moreover, there are still great possibilities of increasing the cultivable area by means of irrigation works. Thus, for example, in Sonora and the Californian peninsula a culture resembling that of U.S.A. California can probably be achieved.

It is further to be noted that Mexico also possesses large unexplored natural resources in other districts. At present only oil is rationally exploited, whilst mining has declined and is only carried on on a relatively small scale. Mexico also offers the further great advantage that, in comparison with the Latin republics of South America, there already exists a fully developed system of transport to the most important centres of production.

Perhaps we can best appraise Mexican potentialities if we compare Mexico's foreign trade with the foreign trade of any other country on the same lattiude with a developed modern civilization. It is natural to think of Cuba in this connection. In 1924 Mexico's imports amounted to 152,000,000 dollars, and exports to 356,000,000 dollars. The population of Mexico is estimated at 15 millions. In the same year Cuba, with a population of only 3 millions, imported goods to the value of 291 million dollars and exported goods of the value of 434 million dollars. The small island of Cuba has actually, therefore, if we look at imports, consumed almost twice as much as Mexico, though its population is only one-fifth as great, and its natural resources, apart from the sun and the fertile soil, are comparatively insignificant. Mr. Chisholm, quoted above, has shown in an interesting study the absurdity in the relation between the capacity of consumption of Mexico and Cuba.[1] In Mexico, he writes, there are about 3 million inhabitants who require to buy imported goods. The remaining population consists mainly of workmen (peons), who may be either Indians or mestizos, and who live at the minimum of existence. They content themselves with a small adobe hut, two or three cotton suits, a sombrero, and the inevitable tortilla or pancake of maize flour and a mug of pulque (a weak alcoholic beverage made from the juice of the maguoy plant). All of these things are produced in Mexico and need not be imported, but if the standard of living of the peon were to be raised things would be different. It is easy to understand the significance of this fact when comparisons are made with Cuba, where we find that the humblest workman eats rice, cod, and preserves, which are imported, and wears cotton clothes

[1] Major H. A. Chisholm, *ibid.*, pp. 4–5.

manufactured abroad. Mexico is one of the world's largest potential markets. In proportion as it is modernized and its requirements increase, even the simplest of its inhabitants will begin to purchase such imported articles as agricultural machinery of all kinds, preserves, cheap decorative articles and musical instruments, gramophones, etc. The Canadian writer even goes further and maintains that if Mexico could develop peacefully for some decades, it would have a population, not of 3,[1] but of 20 million souls, all of whom would be buyers of imported goods.

There is perhaps no exaggeration in the assertion, therefore, that if Mexico's natural resources were ever the object of intensive culture, the country could contribute within a decade to a boom in the whole world, and possibly, owing to its increased general buying capacity, contribute indirectly more than any other country to the reconstruction of Europe.

[1] Three million is the number of inhabitants which, Mr. Chisholm supposes, are now able to purchase foreign goods.

CHAPTER VIII

MUSSOLINI'S EXPANSION POLICY

Italian Colonies and Colonization

ITALY is one of the countries of Europe in which the colonization problem is most acute. From that country there has annually flowed a great stream of emigration both to European and oversea countries. The increase of population in Italy amounts to about 500,000 souls per annum, and the resulting surplus can with difficulty be maintained at home. Italian emigration falls into two groups. The first comprises the so-called seasonal workers, who emigrate to take up casual work in foreign countries in certain months of the year, and remain the rest of the time at home. The second group comprises emigrants who really stay abroad, whether by original intention or by subsequent change of mind. Especially in the south of Italy, there are also a number of emigrants who remain abroad for a period of years and then return with accumulated capital and settle down as small rentiers. A considerable number of such emigrants have returned home, lost their savings, and emigrated again, repeating the process, in some cases, several times.

If one deducts the returned emigrants, Italian emigration still shows a large net excursus, amounting in recent years to 2–300,000. The difficulties encountered by the Italian Government in finding room for this surplus population become greater every year. The restriction of the rights of Italians to immigrate into the U.S.A. has provided yet another drag. The last reduction of the Italian quota has had the effect that whereas in 1922–23 there were 42,845 emigrants, in 1924–25 there were only 2,248. At the same time various other oversea countries have introduced restrictions or regulations which prevent unlimited emigration from Italy.

The increase of population has always been very rapid in Italy. Mussolini himself emphasizes in an interview in the "Svenska Dagbladet" that he regards birth-control as an error of Malthus. He expressed himself very emphatically on the population question in a great political speech in Milan, when he said, among other things:

"The Italian people are all too fertile. I am glad of it. I shall never encourage birth-control. The fact that other countries have fallen into a decline should make us proud of our flourishing increase. Our births exceed our deaths annually by 440,000 in this little peninsula of 40 million inhabitants. These figures show the problems which confront us.

"According as our population increases there are three outlets: To condemn ourselves to voluntary sterility—and Italians are too intelligent for that; to wage war; or to place our surplus population elsewhere."

With such views as his starting-point it is Mussolini's task to find new markets for Italian industry and to acquire the necessary territory for exploitation, whether abroad or in Italy. Mussolini speaks of an "emigrazione interna," by which he means that there are in Italy various districts which by war, declining population, general decay, malaria or other diseases, have fallen into neglect. Sardinia, parts of Sicily and Calabria are among them. But the possibilities of cultivation in these districts are very limited. It is conceivable that Italy might cope with its surplus population without emigration if it had the natural advantages necessary to the creation of an industry capable of producing cheaper than other countries. But Italy does not possess these advantages. It certainly possesses skilled and cheap labour, but it lacks other essentials, especially a supply within its own frontiers or its own colonies of the most important raw materials on which modern material civilization is founded.

These indispensable raw materials of modern material civilization are coal, petroleum, minerals, and rubber. The first three are the foundation of all, and in proportion as the richest and most easily exploited sources of these are diminished there will be disturbances and changes in the world economy of such magnitude that the principal centres of civilization may be transferred. There are really two countries, the U.S.A. and Great Britain, both Anglo-Saxon nations, which control the richest natural resources of the world in minerals and the most important raw materials. England leads in rubber, the U.S.A. in coal and iron, with England and Germany in the second place. As regards petroleum the U.S.A. leads, with Great Britain in the second place. As regards copper and lead the order is the same. In zinc and silver the U.S.A. are also first, Great Britain comes second, but it is, on the other hand, together with its colonies, the world's greatest producer of gold. Italy lacks all such resources. There is very little iron-ore and no coal at all. The only raw material possessed by Italy to any considerable extent is sulphur.

Italian industry cannot, therefore, be developed beyond a certain point. It is not possible by a one-sided development of industry to establish Italy's economic future, for it must be obvious that in the long run no development can continue contrary to nature. There is therefore no other solution for Italy of the population question than to have recourse to emigration, whether to colonies under Italian sovereignty or to lands under a foreign flag.

The Treaty of Peace of Versailles satisfied, it is

true, the most ardent desire of the Italian people for a natural frontier, but it afforded absolutely no solution of Italy's life-and-death problem, which is, how to maintain its increasing population. Italy acquired no colonies and no mandates. At the same time emigration from Italy was rendered still more difficult by restrictions in the immigration laws of various countries, and especially of the U.S.A.

Mussolini was therefore compelled in this matter to fix his attention on three problems : The development of the colonies already held by Italy, the acquisition of new colonial territories, and the facilitating of Italian emigration to foreign countries. In some cases Mussolini has succeeded by negotiation in achieving relatively favourable results. For example, he has acquired from England the territory round the River Juba in East Africa, and thereby rendered possible a future development of the waste littorals of Somaliland. Less important is the renunciation of the oasis of Jurabub by the Egyptian Government, as it has little economic value. Its importance is only of a military kind. Finally Mussolini has succeeded—of which more later—in recent times in obtaining certain guarantees that Western Abyssinia is to be regarded as an exclusively Italian sphere of interest. On the other hand, his diplomacy has been less successful in the Eastern Mediterranean. Italy, after the war, laid claims to certain parts of Asia Minor, but these were rejected. A number of Italian emigrants have nevertheless found their way there, and to other countries on the shores of the Eastern Mediterranean. At present there exist groups of Italian colonists in Egypt, Palestine, and Syria, and one has the impression that Italy has sought to increase its prestige in these parts at the cost of France. But the results obtained up to the present must be inconsiderable, with the possible exception of the circumstance that the Italian mercantile marine has succeeded in establishing itself in the eastern ports of the Mediterranean.

As regards Italy's present colonies on the North African coast of the Mediterranean, Cyrenaica and Tripoli, they have not hitherto been able to absorb a large number of colonists. Provisionally the emigration question has been solved by emigration to France, especially to the department of Toulouse, whither 200,000 Italians have emigrated in the last years. The North African colonies of Cyrenaica and Tripoli are of very different character. Tripoli is of immense extent, dying away in the sands of the Sahara, and comprising four different regions: firstly the coastal district, with its Mediterranean climate and rich vegetation, called the Catena di Smerraldo, or chain of emeralds. Then comes the Djefara, with its steppes rising up to the mountains, and suitable for olive culture. In this district are situated the great ruins of antiquity, among others the town of Laeptis Magna, now being excavated. Further, Djebeb, the mountain, also adapted to olive culture, and finally Hammada, a stony waste, which nevertheless before it reaches the Sahara is bordered by a belt called Fezzan, consisting of an archipelago of oases. The inhabitants of Tripoli consist at present of Arabs, Berbers, and Tuaregs, about 500,000 in all. Hitherto only about 30,000 Italian colonists have settled there, but there are said to be about 70,000 hectares of good soil ready to receive settlers.

Cyrenaica is a more primitive country, with a population of about 200,000 Arabs, most of them leading a nomadic life. The climate is good, with a plentiful rainfall. The country consists mainly of mountainous land on a projecting peninsula. The climate of the high plateau, as of the coast district, is suitable for Europeans.

The Italian, however, has had great difficulty in dealing with the natives. In Tripoli the Arabs have now been subjected by force of arms, and Mussolini's recent visit must be regarded as an official confirmation of this fact. In Cyrenaica, on the other hand, conditions are still unstable and exploitation is in its infancy. Tripoli will be capable of absorbing 300,000 colonists, and in the remoter future possibly an additional half-million.

The colonies along the east coast of Africa, viz. Eritrea, Somaliland, and Jubaland, are for the present only suitable for capitalistic colonization, in so far as white men, though they may direct operations, they can scarcely do manual work.

A great complication in the colonial situation is the lively consciousness of the Italians that the best parts of the North African coastal districts were lost to them when France took possession of Tunis in 1881. There is scarcely a single politically interested Italian who does not regard this as an injustice. It is not only Mussolini and the Fascists who cast covetous glances on this district. Even the Sicilian priest Don Sturzo, formerly Mussolini's most dangerous opponent as leader of the Catholic People's Party, has expressed himself in similar terms and has regretted that Tunis did not become an Italian colony. Like Mussolini, Don Sturzo declares that Italy, and especially Southern Italy, requires an outlet for its markets around the shores of the Mediterranean. The greater the territory which can be brought under Italian sovereignty and which can be exploited by Italian colonists with Italian money, the more surely will it contribute to a solution of the population question in Italy. In the Fascist Press, as also in recent Italian works of a Fascist political colour, it is maintained in very sharp terms that it will not do to deprive Italy of colonial possessions, for the reason that Italy possesses a larger number of suitable emigrants and a more adaptable population than any other country in Europe.

"Italy, it is true," writes Luigi Villari,[1] "developed into a Great Power at a time when most of the best colonial territories had already been annexed by other Powers. But there are still vast empty spaces in the world crying for population to develop their resources; there are rich colonies belonging to countries whose inhabitants are incapable of turning them to account, or to countries who have no surplus population with which to people them and who can only do so by means of emigrants from Italy herself. Why should not some of these territories be assigned to Italy?"

"No one dreams," he continues, "of going to war against this or that Power, but unless some satisfaction is given to Italy's aspirations towards colonial expansion a cause of international unrest will remain."

"An equitable adjustment of the colonial problem would be advantageous not to Italy alone. The whole civilized world needs the development and cultivation of the vast fertile empty spaces still existing in the various continents, more and more as the pressure of population increases, and more food, more fibrous plants, more minerals are required. In the present temper of the Italian nation it would no longer be enough to admit a certain number of Italian workers to foreign countries where they would be gradually denationalized and lost to their mother-country. A different solution is needed, and will certainly be found, as Italy can afford to wait until the justice of its claims and the advisability of satisfying them is recognized by other Powers in the common interest."

To France, with its own colonies in Tunis, Algeria, and Morocco, such a policy cannot be agreeable, as there is always the risk of a conflict of interests. For the moment the danger would not seem to arise, and it appears as if the Abyssinian question has

[1] Luigi Villari: "The Fascist Experiment," Faber & Gwyer, Ltd., London, 1926, pp. 244–5.

been decisive. At the meeting at Rapallo in 1925 between Chamberlain and Mussolini certain agreements were arrived at, according to which England declared that it had no objections to the construction of a railway from Massana to Addis Abeba. This railway, which would run right across Abyssinia, is designed to connect Eritrea with Italian Somaliland. At the same time the whole of Western Abyssinia is to be declared exclusively an Italian sphere of interest. France, which was formerly in strong opposition to this claim of Italy, appears to have given way. Presumably Italy has had to give an undertaking not for the present to threaten the North African colonies of France. To what extent this agreement may be regarded as a real guarantee for the future is another question.

Mussolini has done a great deal to create a possibility of maintaining the surplus population, and the Italian State has taken the matter in hand. In the first place he has devoted his attention to the expansion of native industries, in order to secure employment at home, and at the same time he has sought to capture new markets abroad for Italian goods. Mussolini has established a national institute for foreign trade in order to watch over questions of this kind, though, as I have pointed out in another connection, it is impossible to advance along this path beyond a certain point, as Italy in many respects lacks the essential resources of a leading industrial country.

The emigration question, however, is all the more pressing on that account. In connection with this question Mussolini founded in 1921 an institute for colonial enterprise abroad, in the shape of a limited company of which the capital is subscribed by shipping companies, banks, and other interests. Above it stands the so-called emigration commission, presided over by the Commissary-General for Emigration. This post is held by Professor Michelis, with the present title of ambassador, who both at home and abroad has been warmly approved for his skill and energy. Even the U.S.A. Ministry of Labour and Emigration has expressed the view concerning the Italian emigration commission "that if all countries had such an energetic commission as Italy, there would not be any need for the numerous rules and prescriptions for the regulation and control of immigrants into the United States."

There is no doubt that Italy has set to work more seriously than any other European country to grapple with the problem of emigration and colonization, especially in a practical sense, in so far as it has done so much officially to assist intending emigrants. Thus, for example, special and technical courses of instruction in vocational subjects have been instituted for emigrants, the number of which in the whole country amounted to 288 in 1926. The purpose of these courses is to give to the potential emigrant instruction in the various vocations, with special regard to the capacity of the various workers. The method is specially planned to impart to the emigrant such knowledge as can be illustrated by practical experiments. The courses have been well attended, and care has been taken to make them as flexible as possible in order that an emigrant may begin a course at any time. At attempt is also made to vary the curriculum according as a demand for labour in any particular branch makes itself felt in the foreign labour market. The purely technical courses are directly subject to the Commissary-General for Emigration as being a part of the special vocational instruction which is under his control.[1]

There exists at present a certain amount of rivalry between Rome and Geneva, in so far as Rome seeks to assume the leadership in such important international questions of migration, and Geneva considers that they should be referred to the International Labour Bureau and its subordinate Emigration Committee. When Geneva hesitated what initiative to take, Mussolini hastened as early as May 1924 to hold an international conference in Rome on immigration and emigration problems. Most civilized countries were represented, Sweden also sending an official representative. The congress passed a number of resolutions

[1] International Labour Office Monthly Record of Emigration, No. 46, July 1926, Geneva, 1926, p. 268 *et seq.*

affecting uniform legal definitions in emigration questions and propounded certain desiderata as to greater uniformity in the treatment of emigrants in foreign countries. But the congress also had a higher purpose. Mussolini wished to explore the ground for a project to establish in Rome a national institute for emigration questions, resembling the international agricultural institute which is already organized with its seat in the Eternal City, as an expression of Mussolini's purpose of transforming the Italian capital into a centre for various important international endeavours.

The emigration conference, of which the abovementioned Professor Michelis was president, gave rise, however, to bad blood in the International Labour Bureau in Geneva, which had organized a subsidiary Emigration Committee, although it had not yet taken the initiative in any matter of importance. The Labour Bureau saw in the Italian conference an unwelcome competitor. Italy, however, held the trump card in the fact that the U.S.A. had been officially represented at Rome and the U.S.A., which is not a member of the League of Nations and is therefore not represented in its politico-sociological section, naturally cannot participate officially in the annual general conference of the International Labour Bureau. It is still uncertain whether Mussolini's projected Institute for Emigration Problems will materialize, and recently the opposition between Geneva and

Rome on this question is reported to have abated somewhat. The proposed adjournment of the Rome conference to Havanna in 1927 has been postponed to 1928.

At present Italy is endeavouring to direct its emigration movement along two channels. One leads to its own colonies, but the number of emigrants which can obtain a livelihood in them is still comparatively small and probably cannot be much increased, unless Italy succeeds in the next few years in acquiring suitable territory. The second channel leads, as before the war, to the great oversea countries, but especially to North and South America. As the U.S.A. have now introduced severe restrictions on emigration, the Italians have concentrated their attention more and more on the Argentine and Brazil. Large-scale emigration has also been attempted to various other Latin-American countries, such as Mexico, though up to the present Italy has not been able to organize any considerable stream of emigration in that direction.

As to the Argentine, the number of emigrants has been considerable, the gross figures in 1923 having been 92,000, and in 1924, 73,000. But Italian emigration even to the Argentine has not assumed such proportions as may be regarded as a solution of the problem. Yet from time to time there are reports of Italian emigration experiments in the Argentine and other Latin-American states which appear to be founded on sound principles and to be so extensive as to merit further attention. Thus, for example, in "The Review of the River Plate" of 16th April 1926 there is a report of an Italian enterprise in the Rio Negro valley, called the Compania Italo Argentina de Colonizacion. It was founded in 1924, and the books at the end of the year 1925 show a successful beginning. The organization was mainly established by the Italian Chamber of Commerce in Buenos Ayres, although it has taken no official action. The company commenced operations in October 1924 with a capital of 1,400,000 dollars, most of which was used for the purchase of 5,000 hectares of land in the Rio Negro valley. During the first half-year the company colonized 1,300 hectares, which were divided up into lots of 5, 10 and 15 hectares. These lots have been cleared and ploughed and dwellings have been provided.

In this first stage the company gave preference to Italians who had already resided for some time in the Argentine. The next area to be cultivated consisted of 1,200 hectares, and is at present being partitioned. This section is reserved for Italian families desiring to emigrate from Italy, and these families are selected by an agent of the company on the spot. Work in both districts is in full swing, a water-supply has been laid down, and cultivation has begun. About 1,000 persons have definitely settled on the company's property.

A school, a hospital, a church, a library, and a sports club have been built. The Rome bank founded on Mussolini's initiative to support Italian workmen has contracted to grant a credit to the company of 5 million lira. This undertaking is not indeed large, but it is considered to have started in a manner which may serve as a model for such colonizing activity in general.

An enterprise of greater dimensions is at present planned for Brazil, in so far as the Italian and Brazilian Governments are said to have come to an agreement as to a common colonization plan. The interesting point about this scheme is that it is to be financed by American bankers. It is the first time to my knowledge that American capitalists have displayed any interest in European colonization schemes, but it is highly desirable that this scheme, if it materializes, should be successful and should give rise to the granting of similar considerable credit facilities to other enterprises of a like kind. Much of the capital which Americans have placed, and still endeavour to place, in Europe, either in the form of deposits in European banks, or for the purchase of bonds or industrial shares, would be of much greater use if it were employed instead in carefully prepared enterprises in oversea countries, where new markets for the industry of the world can be developed.

To return to the Italo-Brazilian undertaking, the following particulars may be given. Brazil has undertaken to grant tax-free land for three years, Italy to send the necessary colonists, and the American banks to advance 7 million dollars for the purchase of agricultural machinery, seed, etc. After three years the undertaking is to be subject to ordinary Brazilian taxation and repayment of the bank loan is to begin. An alternative proposal which is under discussion is that some of the Italian shipping companies should guarantee the American loan. In this case the Italian shipping companies would be granted a transport monopoly, both for colonists and materials, as a condition of the guarantee. An emigration of 2–300,000 colonists is estimated, who would establish block settlements in the ceded Brazilian area and would thus constitute a closed Italian colony.

If Italy is to succeed in solving its emigration problem by sending its surplus population to countries under a foreign sovereignty, much depends upon the spirit shown by the states receiving the Italian colonists. At present there prevails, not only in the U.S.A. and most British colonies, but also in the Latin-American states, a strong antipathy to block settlements of foreign nationality. It is desired, on the contrary, that all emigrants should as quickly as possible lose contact with their mother countries in order to become citizens of their adopted country. The projected Italo-Brazilian project is one of the few proposals of recent years in which one-sided nationalistic feelings have not prevented the retention of the national characteristics of the immigrant.

Much would be gained if in Latin America, as well as in Australia and other British colonies, a more liberal attitude were to develop concerning the right of foreigners to collect in larger groups. In oversea countries one need not fear that this would lead to a breaking away of these territories from the country to which they belong. In proportion to the new country as a whole these foreign groups would always be so inconsiderable that they could never constitute any new *irridenta.* On the other hand there is conceivably a grave risk in the case of colonization nearer home, as for example on the north coast of Africa, where the Italians, not only in their own colonies, but also in other places, form such large groups that they may set up a claim for annexation by Italy.

An interesting argument in this connection is to be found in the well-known American periodical " The World's Work." This periodical raises the question how Italy can best acquire colonies for herself, in other words, how Mussolini can redeem his promise to create a " place in the sun " for his compatriot colonists. There are, says the periodical, in general, two paths to be followed if one wishes to extend one's boundaries. In the history of the United States Texas offers a good example of one of these. The U.S.A. did nothing itself in the matter. But United States citizens emigrated to Texas, acquired control of its land and subsequently made a present of the land to the United States. A large part of the British colonial empire has come under the British Crown in the same manner. The other way to acquire colonies is by Government action, which usually consists of conquest by war. The first method is slower and less risky and is, in modern political phraseology, more respectable than acquisition by war. The United States President, Thomas Jefferson, was quite conscious of this difference in 1791, when the Spanish Governor of Florida invited United States citizens to leave their homes and emigrate to Florida and settle there under Spanish rule. Jefferson wrote the following letter in this connection:

> "This is meant for our people, debtors take advantage of it—and go off with their property. Our citizens have a right to go where they please. It is the business of our states to take measures to stop them till their debts are paid. This done, I wish a hundred thousand of our inhabitants would accept the invitation. It will be the means of delivering to us peaceably what may otherwise cost us a war."[1]

So far the American periodical, which thus maintains that if the Italians have the power to colonize a country with so many Italians that they constitute the majority of the population,

[1] "World's Work," June 1926, New York, pp. 128–9.

they would also be entitled to become the owners of the country itself. The Italians will assuredly remember this American recommendation, but I doubt whether on fuller reflection the Americans would be willing to back up this opinion in practice.

An excellent example is Tunis, which in Italian opinion ought to be Italian. All the conditions assumed by the Americans as a preliminary to annexation by the colonizing state are here present, since the Italian colonists are in a decided majority. According to the census of 1921 the total European population comprised 156,170 souls. Of these only 54,477 were French, mostly military and civil servants. The number of Italian colonists amounted to 84,819. In the town of Tunis alone there were 43,000 Italians, against 22,000 French. It should be added that by special agreement with the French Government Italians in Tunis still retain, by observing certain formalities, their Italian nationality.

According to American conceptions France should in this case voluntarily renounce its colony, just as Spain once renounced Florida. But we can be quite certain that this is something which France will never do, and for that reason there lies here a great danger of future trouble in case Italy should not receive suitable compensation elsewhere and the possibility of an outlet for its surplus population.

It is not to be expected that the League of Nations will find a satisfactory solution of this difficulty.

Italian nationalism is in pronounced conflict with the aims of the League. Italian fascism recognizes as a canon no other principle than sacred egoism. Italy takes no notice of Geneva, but relies on its army and navy as a shield of security. Italy seeks to maintain that it is a proletarian nation which has come too late to market to share in the wealth of the world. The present distribution of that wealth is an injustice which Italy insists on rectifying.

CHAPTER IX

GERMAN COLONIAL POLICY

Colonies or Concessions?

IT seems strange nowadays to speak of German colonial policy, since Germany no longer possesses any colonies, but nevertheless the problem is a real one. The president of the German Reichsbank, Dr. Hjalmar Schacht, has declared, as has been mentioned above, that Germany cannot be saved economically unless it resumes its former colonial activity in one form or another. It is therefore not necessary that Germany should possess its own colonies. The question of political sovereignty or mandates may be postponed until the future, but what cannot be postponed is the necessity of Germany's resuming its cultural and economic activity in colonial countries in order to facilitate the supply of foodstuffs and raw materials for its own industry.[1]

"The Dawes plan," writes Dr. Schacht, "cannot be executed unless at the same time Germany is allowed a

---

[1] Dr. Hjalmar Schacht: "Neue Kolonialpolitik," Druckerei der Reichsbank, Berlin, 1926.

great colonial development. The Allies cannot, in the long run, accept German goods in payment. It is a matter of indifference to Germany whether the export of goods occurs direct and gratis to the Allies or against payment to a third party which transfers the proceeds to the Allies. The result is in both cases the same, i.e. Germany throws the output of an undesirable over-production on the world's market. This over-production must consist of manufactured goods, but Germany is the competitor in respect of these goods of the very countries which are to receive them. In other words, Germany cannot pay its debts by deliveries of iron, metals, toys, china, etc.—not because Germany is unable to manufacture such goods, but because the Allies cannot desire the delivery of such articles either to themselves or to the export markets where they compete in the same lines. Large foreign investments in Germany might for a time render possible such foreign payments, but such development is improbable, and in the long run impossible."

According to Dr. Schacht the Dawes plan can only be carried out on the assumption that, in addition to other means of production and surplus of labour, Germany has also access to cheap colonial foodstuffs and raw materials. But it is just for such commodities that world competition is now so keen, and will become even keener in proportion as developments follow the same course as at present. Germany must therefore devote the whole of its energy to procuring at a low price foodstuffs and raw materials from colonial countries. The profitable conduct of German home production is dependent on the solution of this problem. According to Dr. Schacht, German colonial policy is very closely bound up with the currency problem.

German colonial activity can only prosper on the assumption that in German colonial areas German currency is the medium of payment. Germany must be able to buy its oversea foodstuffs and raw materials without having recourse to foreign currencies. The field of action of the German mark must be extended to the colonial areas which Germany exploits. Such an arrangement would be beneficial in several respects. Thus, for example, the reparation payments under the Dawes plan would be rendered considerably easier.

The colonial question is also of great importance to Germany, in so far as Germany must find a suitable outlet for its surplus population. The difficulties of this problem have been rendered more acute since German minorities have been expelled from their former homes by the operation of the Versailles treaty.

For a long time it was said that Germany, like Great Britain, could best spare industrial workers. Agricultural workers could not be spared. But all that is changed now. The whole mass of people who have migrated from Poland to Germany, amounting to about 1 million souls, consists mainly of agricultural workers.

An important element in the problem is to find the necessary money. How can such a colonization scheme as that sketched out by Dr. Schacht be financed, and what legal form should it assume? Dr. Schacht proposes the foundation of so-called Chartered Companies, i.e. large privileged private undertakings with the constitution of companies. If we examine the difficulties a little more closely it becomes clear that in order to realize such a scheme there is required in the first place a suitable geographical area, in the second place emigrants willing to settle in it, and in the third place sufficient capital to launch the enterprise. The emigrants must consist mainly of agricultural workers or of persons both willing and capable of doing pioneer work in a new country. Dr. Schacht considers that Germany possesses suitable human material for such a purpose, especially by reason of the abovementioned influx of a large number of agricultural workers from Poland.

As regards finance, Dr. Schacht is very optimistic. He is convinced that private capital for the foundation of Chartered Companies should be comparatively easy to obtain, since these companies might yield a satisfactory return in a not too distant future.

There are also other means at Germany's disposal such as to collect by means of the so-called Dawes fund capital which Germany is under an obligation to pay in war indemnities but which cannot technically speaking be transferred abroad. It is uncertain if such capital can be profitably employed in Germany itself. But if, continues Dr. Schacht, Germany could introduce its own currency into certain colonial areas later on, in accordance with the above principles, there should be no objections to using the Dawes fund for exploiting these areas.

Such a plan would be accompanied by several advantages. It may perhaps be objected that investments in colonial enterprises yield a slow return. This objection is of little weight, since the Dawes payments are also extended over a long period, i.e. 60–70 years. Moreover, the placing of Dawes capital in colonial investments would render possible the transfer of reparation payments to the Allied Powers in other and easier ways than can otherwise be devised. At this point several perspectives reveal themselves. It is conceivable that raw materials or foodstuffs produced in German colonial areas, and financed by German means, might be sold, for example, to the U.S.A., and thereby set free foreign funds which Germany could use as a means of payment to other Powers. Possibly also the capital invested in German colonial enterprises might in the future be converted into international bonds and thereby scrip be created which might be accepted as a valid medium of payment by the Allied Powers. This is in substance Dr. Schacht's plan.

Assuming the sympathy of the U.S.A., it seems to me also possible that these colonial enterprises might be financed, with American co-operation, by placing the whole of the future colonial movement as security. In this way capital would be set free in advance which might be of benefit to the Allied Powers.

The possible future German colonial policy has

now been surveyed in its more general aspects both with regard to its objects and its capitalization. If one looks more into detail it is possible that other means may present themselves of financing such a colonial enterprise as Dr. Schacht desires to see founded. It is known that the German Government has undertaken to compensate by loan certain private German colonial undertakings which, as a result of the war, lost their possessions in the old German colonies. According to present regulations these loans are only granted in cases where the undertaking in question repurchases the colonial property appropriated by the Allies. Such loans cannot therefore be employed for the acquisition of new colonial districts. It ought to be possible, however, to make this regulation more elastic. In any case it would certainly be advantageous from the German point of view if these regulations were subjected to revision.

Most of the old colonial companies owned colonial possessions which were very profitable as plantations for all sorts of tropical crops, but were not as rule suitable for white colonization. If, therefore, these districts could be replaced by new ones, suitable not only for the production of the foodstuffs and raw materials of which Germany stands in need, but also capable of receiving to a larger or smaller extent German colonists, the German State would appear to have every reason to consider the whole question afresh.

Dr. Schacht's address on colonial policy, which set forth the above descriptions and reflections, must be regarded as one of the most important contributions to the European reconstruction problem of recent times. The success of the Dawes plan becomes more doubtful every day, and the greatest authorities in the Allied countries have become, assuredly with good reason, more and more sceptical of its success. Dr. Schacht's great merit is that he has shown in a clear and incontrovertible manner that the execution of the Dawes plan is a problem of world economics. Unless it is adapted to broad international developments it cannot lead to any positive result.

The German programme of future colonial policy is, however, still very vague. Dr. Schacht's proposal for the foundation of Chartered Companies is, as is clear from the above account, only an economic theory. How the plan would work out in practice Dr. Schacht has not even suggested. He does not indicate which districts he regards as suitable for this proposed colonization scheme, and it is difficult at the moment to see where German colonies of the type he describes could be established.

It is conceivable that Germany, which is now a member of the League of Nations, may recover one or more of her former African possessions. But both England and France have made declarations which suggest that they regard the mandates they have received, not as temporary, but as permanent commissions. In the South African Union hopes are entertained that the British East African colonies will combine in a new republic of " United East Africa," and this new state would then include also the former German Tanganyika territory. It is also certain that the South African Union would not forgo the territory taken over from Germany in the west. It is equally improbable that France would do so unless the present political constellation in Europe is completely changed.

In Germany there are two lines of thought concerning future colonial policy. According to the first, Germany should demand the restitution of the old German territories under a mandate, a plan considered to be of great advantage both economically and politically. The most prominent advocate of this view is the former Governor of German East Africa, Dr. Heinrich Schnee, who has recently published in English a work in defence of German colonial policy before the war, in which he emphasizes Germany's great civilizing influence in this field.[1]

Schnee has many followers in Germany, who have sought to prove by investigation that Germany has the greatest possible interest in recovering these colonies, because she could import from them the greater part of the foodstuffs and raw materials

[1] Heinrich Schnee: " German Colonization, Past and Future," with introduction by William H. Dawson. George Allen & Unwin, London, 1926.

necessary to her industry and to the feeding of her population. Erich Obst, for example, in an article entitled "We demand back our Colonies,"[1] sets forth statistics for 1924 and seeks to prove by their help that the old German African colonies would even now be in a position to export a considerable portion of the tropical goods required by Germany, such as wax, tropical woods, rubber, coffee, cocoa, sisal, and superphosphates. If Germany could employ its own currency in its mandated colonies at the same time as they were exploited with German capital, Germany could buy cheaply all these important raw materials, whilst at present she must buy them from the colonies of foreign countries at prices dictated by them.

Many German experts, however, hold a different opinion concerning the colonial problem, and insist that mandated colonies would at present prove too costly for Germany. Much capital would be required for their exploitation, and it is not conceivable that even with very good management they would yield any substantial return within ten years. The acquisition of mandates would therefore in their opinion burden rather than ease Germany's economic position. All interested Germans, however, must agree with Dr. Schacht that Germany has a great need for providing new homes overseas for her surplus population. It should

[1] Erich Obst: "Wir fordern unsere Kolonien zurück," "Geopolitik," March 1926, p. 157.

be noted, however, that this need cannot be satisfied by the old German African colonies, since they are not suitable under present conditions for white colonization on a large scale. The question of colonization by emigration is therefore a problem quite distinct from that of mandated colonies.

To an outsider it would appear that the most important thing for Germany is to acquire in tropical or other oversea countries districts into which the broad stream of German emigration can be led. Such colonies, which need only be concessions, without sovereign rights, must afford room not only for German scientists and technical experts, but also for agricultural workers and their like. At present, investigations are in progress in many places to discover where such German colonies, or more correctly block settlements, can be established. There are great possibilities both in Mexico and in most of the Latin states of South and Central America. The only question is whether a satisfactory agreement can be concluded between the respective Governments and sufficient capital be found for launching the enterprise.

The Germans appear to be principally interested in the possibilities of colonization in the Argentine, Peru and Chile, which countries were visited by the former Chancellor, Dr. Luther, in the autumn of 1926, for the purpose of study. Similar investigations are in progress in Colombia, where the Government is said to contemplate the transfer of considerable areas in the form of concessions. In the Press there have been mentioned the names of several large companies which have been constituted to take over such concessions, such as " La Companiá General de Negocios, S.A." in Barranquila, and " La Companiá de Colonización de la Sierra Nevada," of which the latter company plans colonization, designed principally for German and Italian families. To all appearances, however, all these colonization plans, with the object of promoting any considerable emigration from Central Europe or other European states, would appear to be still in the initial stages.

German emigration is at present very small. The net emigration in 1925 amounted only to 29,687 souls. This, it is true, is a little more than in the previous year, but it is in any case a figure, as may easily be seen, which in no wise corresponds to actual requirements.[1]

[1] International Labour Office, " Monthly Record of Emigration," Geneva, August 1926, p. 318.

CHAPTER X

THE BRITISH EMIGRATION PROBLEM

Birth-Control and World Politics

GREAT BRITAIN since the war is in a very difficult position owing to considerable over-population. It is therefore more urgent for Great Britain than for any other country to organize comprehensive emigration in combination with the same kind of colonial activity as has continued since immemorial times, and which in practice amounts to a transformation of potential resources into actual wealth,

After the Napoleonic wars Great Britain built up the proud Empire which now comprises an area of 34,596,370 square kilometres, whilst the mother-country, the so-called British Isles, excluding the Irish Free State, is no more than 245,099 square kilometres.

If we glance at the distribution of population throughout the different parts of the Empire, we find how unevenly and sparsely the whole population is still distributed over this vast area. The fact that the colonies accommodate a relatively large population, comprising in all 450 millions, is in this case only a disadvantage, for this population is mainly coloured. And it is clear that the great predominance of this colonial population constitutes an ever-threatening menace to the existence of the scant white population. The distribution of the white population settled in the British Isles and the rest of the Empire is at present approximately as follows:

	Millions.
Great Britain and Northern Ireland	44·2
Irish Free State	3·5
Canada	8·8
Australia	5·5
New Zealand	1·3
South Africa	1·6
India and Crown Colonies	2·1
	67·0

From this table it appears that in spite of their immense area the British possessions do not accommodate more than a third of the total population of the small British Isles.

Australia and New Zealand, which are included in the above table, have practically no coloured inhabitants. New Zealand has an area of 266,542 square kilometres, corresponding to 314,180 square kilometres in Great Britain and Ireland. New Zealand is thus not much smaller than the mother-country, but its population is only 1,300,000 souls.

Still more striking is the disproportion if one looks at Australia, which with a population of something over 5 millions has an area of no less than 7,615,548 square kilometres. Its population is less than an eighth of that of Great Britain, but its area is more than twenty times as great.

Owing to geographical and climatic conditions the new continents are not capable in proportion to their area of maintaining nearly so large a white population as do the European states, but even making large allowances for their unsuitability as homes for the white races, yet it appears abundantly clear that the distribution of population on our planet is very uneven. The density of population is as a rule not in proportion to the productive capacity of the populated areas.

Hitherto the United States have absorbed the bulk of Europe's surplus population ever since the foundation of the great republic in 1776. Emigration only assumed really large dimensions in the middle of the nineteenth century, but it may be said without exaggeration that the emigration from Europe to America during the nineteenth century is in importance equal to that great redistribution of the population of the globe which occurred in the days of the great migration of the peoples.

The emigration which took place to the British colonies in the same period was comparatively inconsiderable, whilst immigration into the U.S.A. amounted to no less than 35 millions, practically all from Europe, and to a very large extent from Great Britain. This emigration has occasioned a complete transformation in the economy of the world. Without this immigrant population, which energetically developed the rich natural resources of the United States, the great republic would still be a waste and the whole of the economic and industrial development which has taken place since 1850 would probably never have occurred in its present dimensions.

After the Great War Great Britain realized the importance of organizing a great stream of emigration, and Parliament voted by the Empire Settlement Act of 1922 a sum of £3 millions per annum for 15 years (£1,500,000 for the first year) in order to promote emigration to the British oversea possessions. In order to assist in the execution of this plan the Overseas Settlement Committee was appointed in 1923 to study and discuss all relevant matters, but it soon appeared in practice that the results did not come up to expectations. During the first three budget years the Government had at its disposal for the purpose £4,500,000, but only spent £460,000, and instead of the expected 80,000 persons per annum who should have emigrated to the colonies under the Act, during the year 1923–24 only 55,000 availed themselves of its provisions.

The dominions and colonies also gave the proposal a somewhat cold reception when it was put into operation. Western Australia, which had undertaken to receive 75,000 persons, had only accepted 4,394 on the 1st of May 1924. New South Wales, which promised to take 6,000, had received none at all. To Canada, which has always shown a strong desire to attract colonists to its unexploited provinces, very few had emigrated. According to the Empire Settlement Act of 1922, emigration to Australia should amount to 450,000, including 35,000 families, averaging 5 heads in each, in the next 10 years. It may appear that this figure is somewhat high, but the emigration of half a million in 10 years is not so great if one remembers that Great Britain has a population of 185 to the square mile, whilst Australia has only 0·77.

Great Britain's emigration policy shows also that emigration since the war has had a tendency to fall off rather than to increase. The following comparison between the years 1913 to 1925 is illuminating:

	Net Emigration.
1913	329,073
1922	119,162
1923	252,776
1924	117,874
1925	113,734

If one examines the destination of these emigrants from Great Britain to various countries and continents it will be found that in 1925, 54,898 went to the U.S.A.; 38,622 to British North America;

35,006 to Australia; 11,730 to New Zealand; 7,004 to South Africa; and 12,365 to India and Ceylon. The result is seen to be somewhat depressing.

In 1923 a delegation was sent out to Australia, New Zealand and Canada in order to discuss colonization plans with the respective Governments. The result was clearly negative, although the delegation in its report supplied useful hints for the practical conduct of large colonization plans.

The delegation had in many cases great difficulty in persuading the authorities in the self-governing dominions of the importance of the proposed emigration. The objection was often raised that the British Government was seeking to reduce unemployment at home by sending out as many unemployed as possible, without regard to their suitability for life in the colonies. It was also an indisputable fact that the colonies required agricultural workers as settlers and the mother-country had no such workers to spare. The emigrants must undertake not to seek work in the towns, a demand which was the more natural, since even in the new countries a tendency to move from the country to the towns was already making itself felt.

Another difficulty was the increasing specialization of function among European workers. There are plenty of clerks, mechanics, machinists and other technically trained people, but it is difficult to find people who know how to till the soil and do the coarse joinery work which is required in the colonial wastes. In the emigration of the 'fifties people emigrated simply because they could not get a livelihood at home. They went primarily to the U.S.A., but nobody inquired how they thrived there. It is certain that only the fittest survived; many went under, but nobody cared. Nowadays nobody will run such risks. The emigrant demands an organization to assist him and to finance both his own and his family's journey and their work on arrival.

Such an organized emigration scheme as the Empire Settlement Act presupposed requires a large capital, an extensive organization and intimate co-operation between the mother-country and the colonial Governments. The goal must be really attractive or otherwise no English workman will emigrate, largely owing to the unfortunate trend of English unemployment and poor-law policy since the war. Most workmen prefer to live a restricted but care-free life at home to exposing themselves to the unknown in oversea lands. No propaganda can overcome such reluctance, and the British Committee is therefore forced to the conclusion in its report that the only possibility of a positive result is to make the prospects for emigrants as attractive as possible. "A contented settler," it says, "is the best magnet for attracting others."

The Oversea Settlement Committee has investigated conditions of emigration in former times in order thereby to elucidate the factors which may have a stimulating effect. The Committee states among other things that emigration tends to decline in times of bad business, but is increased in good times. As early as 1885 Sir Robert Giffen wrote:[1] taken as a rule the volume of emigration is inconsiderable during periods of bad trade, but increases in a period of good trade immediately succeeding bad times. The probable cause is that emigration has hitherto been principally to the United States. It is therefore the boom in that country which has determined the volume of emigration from Europe. But it is obvious that the commercial conditions in the U.S.A. react on the European situation, and it is therefore natural that the volume of emigration from Europe should be greater in good years than in bad. But in point of fact it is not favourable business position in Europe which causes increase or decrease of emigration, but the position in the United States or other countries to which emigration takes place, which is really the determining factor.

Sir Robert Giffen's opinion doubtless holds now just as much as in former times. It is the conditions in the country of destination which must attract the emigrant, whilst conditions in the country which he leaves are of less importance.

[1] See "Report of the Oversea Settlement Committee," December 1925, p. 20.

Since the restriction law of the U.S.A. was introduced, these conditions can no longer determine the volume of emigration from Europe. But it is clear that free capital in large amounts must be available in the countries to which emigration takes place. And since Europe now lacks such capital and is not in a position to create in the emigration country the favourable conditions which are the necessary preliminary to successful colonization, such capital must be raised in some other way. As things are at present no solution of this world problem of colonization would appear possible without effective financial assistance from the United States.

Since, however, Great Britain came to recognize after the war the great difficulties in the way of comprehensive colonization, other proposals for the solution of the problem have also been made in public discussion of the matter. In the first place the question of voluntary birth-control has become acute in England.

To what extent the birth-rate can be voluntarily regulated depends on the views commonly held on this subject. Before the war discussion of this matter on the present scale would have been unthinkable, but times have changed. The Great War and its effects have convinced mankind that something drastic must be done.

Certain conditions and episodes of the war forced both the authorities and public opinion to concern itself with this question in a manner without parallel in the past. Thus, for example, the Australian Government threatened to discontinue all recruiting if extraordinary measures were not taken as a protection against venereal disease.

In Great Britain expert authorities have conducted widespread publicity on this subject, especially Mrs. Marie Carmichael Stopes. Her writings and the manner in which her views have attracted attention in public discussions constitute one of the most striking pieces of evidence of how radically opinions have changed on this subject. Her versatility is amazing, and she touches in her works on the most varied subjects. Thus, for example, she has written important works on botany, works of travel, poems, tragedy, as well as a very valuable history of the drama in old Japan. But best known are her works on birth-control and related questions. She has raised the whole discussion of this problem, which the English call contraception, to a higher social plane than any previous advocate has achieved.

It is a significant fact of historical interest that when she was recently presented at Court her portrait was published in one of the weekly illustrated journals, among a number of other débutantes, with the added inscription "of birth-control fame." We wonder what would have been said of this in the reign of Queen Victoria.

One of her fundamental works, "Wise Parenthood,"[1] a piece of propaganda which has had an immense circulation, begins with a quotation from a letter from Queen Victoria to the King of the Belgians, dated 15th January 1841:

> "I think, dearest Uncle, you cannot *really* wish me to be the 'Mamma d'une nombreuse famille,' for I think you will see the great inconvenience a *large* family would be to us all, and particularly to the country, independent of the hardship and inconvenience to myself. Men never think, at least seldom think, what a hard task it is for us women to go through this *very often*."

It is characteristic of Mrs. Stopes that she should thus link her agitation to a period of modern English history which would certainly have been quite incapable of understanding her ideas. Opinions have, however, changed so much since then that even the Anglican Church has seriously occupied itself with the problem, though the Catholic Church, true to its traditions, has taken up a position of unbending opposition.

> "Morally, as well as eugenically," writes the Bishop of Birmingham in "The Times," 1919, "it was right for people in certain circumstances to use harmless means to control the birth-rate. . . . It was immoral to avoid having children from selfish motives, but it was surely also immoral to have child after child under circumstances which, humanly speaking, were such as to render the proper upbringing of such children impossible."

The Catholic Church is carrying on a vigorous

[1] Marie Carmichael Stopes: "Wise Parenthood," G. P. Putnam's Sons, London, 1921, p. 1.

propaganda against Mrs. Stopes and her disciples. The question of contraception was discussed, for example, at the National Catholic Congress in Manchester in 1926, and the opinions there expressed were very characteristic, in so far as the Catholics clearly view this question in the same light as those unpenalistically minded states which regard an increased population as a spur to the expansion of territory. The Catholic Church does not desire warlike conquests, but it urges what one might call a religious imperialism and hopes by means of prolific families to gain ground at the expense of other churches. Thus, for example, at the above congress Lady Elwes said:

> "In these days, when some people talk about race suicide, Catholic women should allow themselves to be led by the authority and principles of the Church and thereby be of great service to their country. Perhaps the England of the future may be ruled by Catholics, just because they will continue to bear children, whilst those of other faiths will cease to bear them."

The present agitation for birth-control in Great Britain is concerned primarily with the question how best to organize effective propaganda among the poorer classes, and it has been proposed that the Ministry of Health should take the question of contraception in hand and carry on suitable propaganda. There are already a number of private institutions which supply information on the subject. Especially the Malthusian League, with its branches at Woolworth and Kensington, have done much work. To this must be added the propaganda conducted by Mrs. Stopes herself, especially in the poorest districts of London, in which she has the assistance of a number of eminent collaborators. Moreover, Dean Inge, who is also well known in Sweden, has strongly advocated the dissemination among the lower classes of a knowledge of suitable methods of contraception. He states that there is at present a lamentable ignorance of the subject, and in its place there is much procuring of abortion, whilst wilful neglect of new-born children is a very common occurrence. His conclusion is that it is the duty of society to spread a knowledge of the subject in all classes of the community.[1]

If one looks at the English literature on the subject it cannot be denied that in some cases it exaggerates in bad taste. Not especially attractive, for example, is the attitude taken up by the Oxford tutor, Haldane, in his well-known work "Daedalus."[2] His starting-point is that it will be scientifically possible completely to separate procreation and sexual love, and, in his way of thinking, set mankind free and make it better in an entirely new sense. He conceives future child-bearing as mainly

[1] William Ralph Inge: "England," Ernest Benn, London, 1926. Cf. e.g. pp. 200, 208 and 286.

[2] T. B. S. Haldane: "Daedalus, or Science and the Future," Kegan Paul, London.

a process of so-called " ectogenesis," or as what one might call a sort of chicken-farming on scientific principles. Cohabitation of man and wife would, as it were, be independent of the question of children, a view which to some extent corresponds to Mrs. Stope's principal thesis, which is not the restriction of population in the ordinary sense. Views similar to those of Haldane, though not so advanced, are put forward by the well-known Cambridge mathematician Bertrand Russel in his pamphlet " Icarus, or the future of Science."[1] He maintains, among other things, that the time is near when the Governments of various countries will permit the generation of just so much human material as is required for their special needs. The realization of such scientific dreams would transform mankind into a sort of Ford motor-works.

Experience shows us that if mankind does not voluntarily confine the procreation of children within proper bounds, nature herself will see that the population is reduced. But the limitation effected in this way is of the most unpleasant kind, and it is therefore highly desirable that mankind should by its own efforts prevent nature's course or alleviate its effects

Only two methods of limiting or reducing the population are conceivable: one by nature and the other by voluntary abstention. Nature's method,

[1] Bertrand Russel: " Icarus, or the Future of Science," Kegan Paul, London.

which has hitherto prevailed, consists in catastrophic crises, which arrive of their own accord and visit mankind with terrible suffering, as in the case of war and its consequences, plagues and disease. These are the only methods employed by nature. The other method is voluntary limitation of births, and consists of a systematic lowering of the birth-rate in order to avoid over-population.

The world situation has never been so critical for mankind as at present. Progress in hygiene and medical science have had the effect that whilst child mortality decreases the span of life increases. Epidemics such as smallpox, plague, cholera, diphtheria, scarlet fever, and syphilis, which in former times reduced the population, are now either stamped out or reduced as a result of the progress of medical science or of better hygienic conditions in general. The same effect is produced by the numerous charitable and other humanitarian institutions which have been introduced by modern social legislation and which help to preserve the weak and the unfit. The most striking example on a large scale is to be found perhaps in English rule in India. The cessation of the earlier internecine war between the small states, the elimination of epidemics and famine, etc., have had the result that in the last ten decades, i.e. since British Government rule superseded that of the British East India Company, the population of India has increased by more than a hundred millions, that is to say by an amount equal to about the whole population of the United States.

Nowadays it can scarcely happen in Europe that a person starves, however worthless he may be. A number of persons who for reasons of bad health or from other physical causes ought to die young are now artificially kept alive, and as if that were not enough, they often bring forth unsound descendants, who constitute a renewed burden on the community.

Among the uncivilized races quite different conditions prevail. Natural selection is still the rule, eliminating the weaker strain. In modern society, on the other hand, drunkards and other worthless creatures are permitted without hindrance to marry and bring children into the world, often as many as possible, or, more correctly, as long as the wife's health lasts.

The middle classes in almost all European countries, and especially in Great Britain, have a strong sentiment of class ambition. A man who has been educated in a certain tradition wishes to give his children a similar education, and if by reason of increased taxation or a higher cost of living he is unable to give them an education such as he has had himself, he prefers to limit the number of his family rather than have children to whom he fears he cannot give a good start in life. Such is the reasoning of everybody who has a feeling of responsibility for his family and children. This responsibility has been increased since the war. Times are troubled and nobody knows what the morrow will bring forth. The world as it is appears to many parents an unsuitable place for a large family. It may be added that this view is also common in the ranks of skilled labour, but if one goes farther down in the social scale other conditions are found to prevail—perhaps especially in England, where the payment of unemployment relief has had most demoralizing effects. The consequence has been that lower-grade manual labourers, persons without any real occupation, the permanently unemployed or other unemployables, have become entirely indifferent both to their own fate and to that of their families. Many of them desire as many children as possible because for each child they receive more support from the public coffers. They feel nothing of the restraint and sense of responsibility to be found in the middle classes, and perhaps also in wide circles of skilled labour.

Published statistics throw a vivid light on the unsuitable birth-rates of the various classes of society. If one goes back to the census for Great Britain of 1911, it will be found that the number of births per 1,000 married men under 55 years of age was 162, whilst the corresponding figure for the upper classes was only 119. The birth-rate of children per 1,000 families under 55 in the various trades and professions appears from the following table:

Anglican priests	101
Other priests	96
Teachers, professors, etc.	95
Doctors	103
Authors, publishers	104
Police	153
Post Office	159
Coachmen and chauffeurs	207
Dock workers	231
Waiters	234
Miners	258
Manual labourers, unemployed, etc.	438

This table shows clearly that those worst placed socially have most children. This fact reveals one of the greatest difficulties of the birth-restriction problem, namely, that limitation is not practised by that section of the population of which the reproduction is injurious from the point of view of race biology. The consciousness of this fact has, as already indicated, led to extensive propaganda in England for the dissemination of suitable knowledge among the lower classes, in which mothers as a rule go to their fate with the same submissiveness as soldiers go to their death at the front. As we have seen, the limitation problem bristles with difficulties. From the point of view of the State it is primarily of importance that those families which from the social point of view produce the best offspring should do their duty and not restrict their families too much, and there is always a risk that the less desirable elements of society should produce the most children.

The head of the British Statistical Office has recently commented on the extremely unsatisfactory number of inferior children in England. Those belonging to this group, he says, lack the general ability to profit by their instruction. And the group is so numerous that every year 50,000 new recruits of such a type enter our industrial army. That is to say, 50,000 individuals, who not only by defective psychical development are incapable of meeting effectively the claims of life, but also bring into society the greater part of its useless population of beggars and wastrels.

"There is no equality in nature," writes Sir James Barr, "among children nor among adults, and if there is to be a much-needed improvement in the race, we must breed from the physically, morally, and intellectually fit." [1]

Voluntary restriction of the birth-rate is, however, not a problem which can be considered from the point of view of one country alone, but must be seen internationally, i.e. in association with what happens in other countries. Every country which practises artificial limitation places itself in a worse position internationally than the countries which do not. A result satisfactory to the whole world would presuppose that all countries should limit their population to approximately the same extent, which in the present state of developments is not practicable

[1] Sir James Barr, "British Medical Journal," London, 1918.

Broadly speaking, a limitation of population has occurred in most of the states of northern Europe, such as France, Sweden, Norway, Denmark, Germany, Holland, Belgium, and Switzerland. On the other hand, it is necessary among the South European peoples such as the Spaniards, the Italians, and the Portuguese, among whom the increase is still extraordinarily great. An attitude in strong opposition to every thought of restriction has been taken up by Russia and the Slavonic races, and this refusal is perhaps even more pronounced in Japan, China, and India. All these races regard an increase of population as something unavoidable, or rather obvious. The problem has not yet arisen in their case, and probably for a long time to come any efforts in this direction will be foreign to their ideas.

Professor David Davidson believes [1] that in consequence of birth-control in Europe the neo-Malthusian countries would at the end of 60–70 years have a combined population of 180 millions, more or less, whilst the rest of the world's population would have considerably increased. In elucidation of this view he reminds us that after 1850 the population of the countries above designated as neo-Malthusian increased from 114 to 181 millions, or 50 per cent, whilst in the other European countries it increased from 152 to 279 millions, or 83 per cent.

[1] "Aftonbladet," 10th February 1926.

"If it is true," he continues, "that these countries contain, racially, the world's best populations, it would be simply stupid from the point of view of the whole world to limit their increase, as the rest of the world would simultaneously profit by its potentiality of increase. And if this development could not be prevented it would not be reasonable to characterize it as beneficial."

At this point we arrive at the real crux of the question, i.e. how the neo-Malthusian countries of Europe can impose their views on the rest of Europe and the world, and secure their co-operation. Australia and the United States have already adopted the European view, but India, China, and Japan are in strong opposition. Of these, Japan is the most important state, and it must be admitted that Japan has set its face more firmly than even the Catholic Church against any systematic birth-control, which they condemn both on religious and on national grounds. In Japan loyalty to the supreme head of the State, the descendant of the Sun Goddess, demands that every man should marry and have as many children as possible, especially male children, whom he must educate to preserve the family traditions and to become soldiers. This doctrine is preached in Japan without regard to the resources of the country, and has led in the past to a great stream of Japanese emigration annually to other countries. Since such emigration has now become very much obstructed by the United States prohibition it is obvious that the political tension in the world has been increased, and that especially the relations between Japan and the U.S.A. have been rendered unstable.

It is in the nature of things that unrestricted increase of population in one country must finally lead to war with other countries. So it has been in the past and so it must be in the future. The Great War set free latent forces and revealed the untenability of the present distribution of the population of the globe, and the great dangers of continued increase. For so long as this increase remains uncontrolled we may be sure that similar catastrophes will befall us sooner or later.

The greatest danger is present when the increase occurs in highly civilized states such as Italy and Japan, whilst other equally civilized countries practise a strict birth-control. In countries standing on a lower level of civilization, such as India, the risk of war in the event of dangerous over-population is not so great, owing to the fact that such countries are not provided with an organization enabling them to conduct war on modern lines. The catastrophe therefore assumes a different form in such countries, and in them there also occur repeated famines, causing endless suffering to individuals, though they do not necessarily lead to war. In this connection we may mention the devastating influenza epidemic in India in 1918.

The only real solution of the problem is to convince each people that it must restrict its population to the maximum economically desirable. If this is not done it is clear that no form of international pacificism can prevent the outbreak of new wars in the future when the pressure of population becomes too great. Man will have failed to find a solution, but nature, which is implacable, will continue to solve the problem, as in the past, in her own relentless way.

It is conceivable that a rational solution may be found which may be of advantage to a particular country regarded as a single whole. But even such a solution will only have its effects in the remote future. In this way no improvement can be expected in the next generations. A rapid slackening of the present tension can only be achieved if Europe succeeds in organizing a large-scale emigration, as has been attempted ever since the Great War, though without conspicuous success. Birth-control is a problem by itself, which may be of great importance in the future, but it is the merest humbug if one looks at the present situation.

This is all the more evident since there are at present at least two Great Powers in the world which consistently show by their policy that they consider a large and increasing population to be an asset in the struggle for a place in the sun, namely, Japan and Italy. A diminution of the surplus population of Europe and of its accompanying risks can only be accomplished if the present unemployed surplus is sent out on a mission of peaceful conquest to the still unexploited territories of the world. Not to do so, but to concentrate attention instead on such future internal problems as birth-control is to put a premium on the peoples which, like the Japanese and the Italians, have the strongest will to survive and ask nothing better than to conquer the world at the expense of the races which will not submit to the sacrifices necessary to achieve their object.

CHAPTER XI

THE IMMIGRATION RESTRICTIONS OF THE UNITED STATES

Secret Immigration and the Negro Problem

THE restrictions on immigration introduced by the United States after the war are significant. These restrictions have become progressively more and more severe. The present regulations are operative until 30th June 1927, but after that date it is intended to adopt new principles by which the quota of immigrants to the United States will be still further diminished. The immigration figure will in fact become so small that, at least so far as Sweden is concerned, it will be equivalent to complete exclusion.

The United States fiscal year is reckoned from 1st July in one year to 30th June in the next. During the fiscal year 1912–13 immigration into the United States amounted to 1,197,892 persons, and in the corresponding period of 1913–14 to 1,218,480 persons. Then came the Great War, during which immigration practically ceased. When it was again resumed the Americans sought to confine it by restrictive legislation. To this end the so-called 3 per cent law was introduced in 1921, by which the permitted immigration from each country was limited to 3 per cent of the number of American citizens born in the country in question and included in the American census of 1910. By this law the permitted number of immigrants was 357,807 persons, or a little more than 25 per cent of the normal immigration during the years immediately preceding the war. Within a short time even this reduction will not satisfy the Americans.

They also demand another basis of calculation, not in order to bring down the actual figure, but to restrict the stream of emigration from those European countries whose inhabitants they regard as less desirable settlers. Among such states are included Russia, Poland, and several other eastern European states, and Italy. In order to achieve this purpose the Americans went back to the census of 1890, and by a supplementary law of the 19th of May 1924 they fixed on that census as the foundation of a new census of nationality. At the same time they reduced the percentage figure with which they calculated from three to two.

Before 1890 the immigrants from Europe to the U.S.A. had come principally from northern Europe, and thus consisted of members of the Anglo-Saxon or Germanic race. Immigrants from eastern and southern Europe were still rare. Thus, for example, in the forty years preceding the year 1890 Italy only contributed 324,000 immigrants and Russia 385,000. The great invasion from these two countries did not begin until after 1900, but developed then all the more rapidly. From that date until 1920 Italy sent no less than 3,800,000 immigrants, and Russia 2,100,000. It was this powerful invasion of Latins and Slavs which the Americans sought to stop by the supplementary law of 1924.

The reversion to the 1890 census is of great importance from another point of view than that already mentioned, in so far as the population of the U.S.A. in that year was considerably less than in 1921. A 2 per cent quota of the 1890 population therefore considerably reduced the permitted number of emigrants, and the total was brought down from 357,803 to 164,667, which latter number constituted the emigration quota fixed by law for the fiscal year 1924–25. If one compares this number with the normal number of emigrants before the war, i.e. about 1,200,000 per annum, it will soon be seen how revolutionary the effect of the new American restrictions on Europe must be. Many European states which, like Sweden, sent their emigrants almost exclusively to the United States, find every possibility of placing their surplus population removed. Such states must therefore seek to find other countries willing to receive their emigrants on reasonably satisfactory conditions. The prohibitive effect of the American immigration legislation has not, however, been equally strong in all countries. One of the objects of the return to the 1890 census was to favour Anglo-Saxon immigration, and this purpose was achieved. For the year 1922–23 the immigration quota for Great Britain and Ireland was fixed at 77,342, but for the year 1924–25, when the supplementary regulations came into force, this was cut down to 62,374. In the last fiscal year before the war the number of emigrants amounted to 107,199. The restriction was not, as we see, so great as regards Great Britain, but it was all the greater on that account for other countries. Sweden's quota was reduced from 20,042 to 9,561; Denmark's from 5,619 to 2,789; and Norway's from 12,202 to 6,453. The reductions were even greater, as was indeed intended, in the case of Latin and Slavonic immigration. Italy's quota was reduced from 42,128 to 3,845; Russia's from 24,405 to 2,248; and Poland's from 30,977 to 5,982.

And still the Americans are not satisfied. Still more severe restrictions are to follow. The contention is made that the established calculation should operate until 1st July 1927, after which a further reduction is to ensue, in such a way that the total number of immigrants may be fixed once and for all at 150,000 persons annually. This number is to be distributed among the various nations, not on the 2 per cent basis calculated according to residents in the U.S.A. born abroad, but in proportion to the relation of the population of the U.S.A. to the various national constituents thereof as existing in 1920. The fixing of this percentage, based on origin, was left to a committee of three members of the American Government. To all appearances the selection under the ordinance will leave a certain arbitrary margin.

How emigration will develop in case the quota based on national origin comes into operation is not yet known. Certain calculations have, it is true, been published in the Press, but they are not founded on official information, and they cannot be accepted as anything but approximate. Nothing has yet been decided as to what will happen after 1927. If the present regulations are to be withdrawn, the law prescribes that a list containing the new immigration figures shall be published before 1st April 1927. If this is not done the same rules will apply as at present during the budget year 1927–28. Every rearrangement of the quota must be notified 90 days before the close of the financial year in order to have legal sanction. So long as this is not done the previously existing distribution remains in force.

It is also intended to introduce a stricter control than heretofore of foreigners visiting the United States. Thus, for example, the Minister of Labour has made a proposal that all foreigners in the U.S.A. should annually register themselves in order that it may be determined whether any foreigners are resident contrary to the law and the regulations. In this way it is hoped to check the present free immigration over the frontiers from neighbouring states. This proposal has, however, at the moment of writing not yet become law.

If one looks at the immigration problem from the point of view of the United States themselves, the present regulations can scarcely be regarded as satisfactory. We can understand that the Americans wish to maintain their present high standard of living and do not wish to see an influx of people of the lower races. But on the other hand, they ought not to raise objections to receiving contingents of the Nordic races, and it is not improbable that certain modifications of the law will be adopted which will benefit the Nordic peoples.

It would appear that a restriction of white immigration of such severity as that at present in force would not be of real advantage to American development. Especially we should not forget that the United States have themselves to solve an important race problem within their own frontiers. It is all very well to exclude the yellow races, but the United States has in the negroes a black population which is daily becoming a more and more important factor in the situation. Even before the war the negro question caused much anxiety It is not the case, as is commonly supposed, that the opposition between the white and black races after the war between North and South and the abolition of slavery has become less than formerly, rather is the contrary the case. The negro is still a pariah who is in a sense quite outside the community. On paper the negro has the same rights as the white man, though he may not vote. The suffrage law is such that a certain school education is obligatory before the vote can be exercised, and it has been so formulated that, with few exceptions, the negroes cannot exercise it. Negroes may not travel in the same railway coaches, may not visit the same restaurants and theatres, nor use the same waiting-rooms as the white man.

In the northern states, it is true, the dislike of negroes is not theoretically so strong, but the northerner abominates the odour of the concrete negro. The general opinion is that the opposition between black and white is greater than ever. The position is rendered still more difficult as the negro raised new claims during the war. He was then suddenly in demand, as the workmen who went to the war had to be replaced by black workers. The latter then swarmed from the southern states into the northern states. To Chicago alone there came 100,000 negroes, who remained there, but who are not especially beloved by the white race. The resulting vacuum in the southern states was filled by peons from Mexico, and in this manner the United States received, by another route than immigration from across the ocean, a numerous element of population, which from the point of view of race biology must have been less welcome than even those Europeans who have been described as "less desirable."

From Canada there is also a secret immigration going on depending, as we have already stated, on the fact that the restrictions of the American Immigration Act is partially annulled because people even of alien origin are allowed to immigrate [1] from the countries bordering on the United States and unaffected by this law (Mexico and Canada), if they had been settled there for two years in the one case, five in the other. Thus the total immigration from Canada and Mexico rose from 66,361 for the financial year of 1922 to 290,026 for 1924.

> "The increase of open and secret emigration from Canada and Mexico into the United States," [2] states the "Encyclopædia Britannica," "shows that unless continental migration be regulated, the intentions of legislation regarding overseas migrants will merely be paper regulations."

We must also consider that the negro race is constantly increasing. It is true that the rate of increase of the negro population is not as high as among the whites, but in proportion as the immigration of the latter is reduced the proportional difference between the black and white increase of population will become less marked. The negro population already amounts to an imposing total.

[1] The "Encyclopædia Britannica." The thirteenth edition, New Supplementary Volume II, p. 909.

[2] *Ibidem*, p. 912.

IMMIGRATION RESTRICTIONS OF THE U.S.A.

In 1910 there were in the U.S.A. nearly 8·8 million negroes, but in 1920 the number had grown to 10·5 millions. Although the negroes are principally employed on the land or in mines, yet they play an important rôle in the labour market of the United States. If they become too numerous and better educated than at present, serious conflicts must arise, and the question must also come up for decision whether it would not be wiser by an increase of white immigration to erect a dam against the constantly "rising tide of colour."

CHAPTER XII

CANADA AS AN EMIGRATION COUNTRY FOR THE NORTHERN RACES

AS appears from the preceding chapter, the American restriction laws have caused a great interruption in the stream of emigration to the United States from the north European countries. Even though the reduction of the quota for the Scandinavian countries has not been so great as for many other countries, yet the restriction of emigration has hit those countries hardest, in so far as it has proved very difficult, up to the present, to direct the stream of Scandinavian emigration to other parts of the world. Especially, all attempts to transplant emigrants from northern Europe to tropical countries have failed. The Scandinavian emigration question is a problem by itself which differs from the problems of the other European countries and requires consideration from special points of view. But owing to the great influence exercised by the Scandinavian peoples in the development of the United States, it may not be without interest even to an English reader to know how the Scandinavian countries view this matter. In what follows we shall direct our attention in the main to Sweden, partly because that country has had the largest emigration, and partly because there is a great deal of material available for forming an opinion on the subject. It should be emphasized, however, that the problem is analogous in both Denmark and Norway, especially in the latter country, where prevailing views coincide with those of Sweden.

Whether there exists at present an actual need for emigration it is difficult to say, but it is a fact that there exists a certain desire to emigrate, i.e. a "conventional" need for emigration.

Hitherto the stream of emigration has been almost exclusively to the U.S.A., but on account of the American restriction laws the permitted annual total of emigrants to the United States is at present limited to 9,500 in round numbers for persons of Swedish birth. This figure does not suffice even for the "conventional" emigration. If one counts the applications for a permit which reach the American consulates in Sweden, it will be found that they are so numerous that applicants must wait about eight months before they can expect an answer. From this it follows that applications annually exceed the prescribed quota by an amount equal to about two-thirds of the quota, or about 6,000. If this number is added to the permitted quota, we arrive at a total number of applications annually of about 15,000 emigrants. If to this figure we add the number of Swedes emigrating annually to Canada, numbering about 1,000, we may obtain a fairly accurate idea of the "conventional" needs of emigration, amounting to between 15,000 and 20,000 persons.

In this figure is not included the need for emigration of expert labour, such as that of engineers, foresters, doctors, etc., which of recent years has become more and more pressing, and constitutes a special problem.

The Sweden-Canada question has attracted attention by the fact that the Canadian National Railways opened an Information Bureau in Gothenburg in 1926, of the same type as those previously opened in Copenhagen and Oslo. It may be mentioned in passing that it is forbidden by Swedish law for authorized emigration agents to carry on emigration propaganda. Such an office must therefore operate with the greatest circumspection, but so long as it merely affords information by means of pamphlets or otherwise no objection can be formally made. Nor can it be denied that such information bureaus may be of use to emigrants.

Much depends upon the manner in which such a bureau exercises its functions. According to Professor Gösta Bagge,[1] Canada conducts its propaganda

[1] Gösta Bagge: "Canada as an Emigration Land," Sociala Meddelanden, No. 8, 1925, pp. 619 *et seqq.* See also on Canada, Helge Nelson: "Canada the Pioneer's Land,"

with great care. Its publications are of the very best, and are designed to give the reader a favourable view of the future possibilities of Canada, but it is in the nature of things that the descriptions should be somewhat biased. Positively incorrect statements do not appear, but neither is the whole truth given, and the publications are sometimes misleading in consequence of what they omit to say. The main question is how far Canada can replace the U.S.A. for the placing of surplus labour from Sweden or other Scandinavian countries. Bagge points out that even in Canada opinions on this subject differ considerably. The optimists point out that Canada has an area of 6 million square kilometres, of which 2 millions are fertile, and only 250,000 under cultivation. Canada has also great reserves of forests, water power, minerals, and fisheries, with a population of only 9 millions, which corresponds to only about two-thirds of the combined population of London and Paris. The pessimists in Canada, on the other hand, point out that there is frequent unemployment in Canada, arising from the marked seasonal fluctuations on the labour market. The climate is severe, and well-situated free State land is nowadays scarce.

Stockholm, 1922. Helge Nelson: "The Interior Colonization in Canada at the Present Day and its Natural Conditions," Meddelanden från Lunds Geografiska Institution, Ser. B., No. 11. An excellent account of recent date is given by Ivar Vennerström, Member of the Riksdag, in his book, "Kanada," Tidens Förlag, 1926.

As a noteworthy symptom of an unfavourable kind it is also mentioned that the emigration of Canadians to the U.S.A., especially of youth, often occurs to such an extent that the immigration surplus is sometimes converted into an emigration surplus. Among Swedish settlers in Canada opinions vary in the same way. Swedes who came there twenty or thirty years ago, and are now prosperous farmers or business men, still regard it as a country which offers great advantages to such immigrants as will accept hard work. The younger Swedish immigrants view the situation more pessimistically on account of the bitter experience they have not infrequently had.

When Canada was first colonized in the eighteenth century two main racial groups were distinguishable, i.e. the French settlers who had left their country during the first period of French colonization, and the English loyalists, who after the American War of Independence moved to Canada because they wished to retain their British citizenship.

The artificially stimulated emigration to Canada came quite late and reached its culminating point only after 1900. From the 31st March 1900 until the 31st March 1923 not less than 3,740,197 settlers immigrated into Canada, of which nearly 1½ millions during the four years preceding the war. Then came a considerable decrease, but during the crisis in the years immediately after the war immigration was resumed and rose in the budget year 1924–25 to over 150,000 persons. At the same time there took place emigration from Canada to the U.S.A. to such an extent that the immigration surplus was quite small. Thus, for example, immigration in the years 1911–21 amounted to 1,728,921, whilst emigration in the same period amounted to 1,297,740, leaving a surplus immigration of 431,181.

Before 1890 the emigrants into Canada were principally North Europeans, but later there came a not inconsiderable number of emigrants from eastern Europe, especially Galicia. The Scandinavian population of Canada amounted in 1921 to 167,359 persons, of which there were 61,503 Swedes, 68,856 Norwegians, 21,124 Danes, and 15,876 Icelanders. At the present moment there are estimated to be about 70,000 persons of the Swedish race, corresponding to 0·8 per cent of Canada's total population.

The Great War occasioned in Canada, as in the rest of the world, many changes, among which the most serious from the European point of view was that Canada also began to develop a comprehensive industrial activity, and there arose a considerable drain of the population to the towns, especially among the younger generation. We find here, therefore, the same development as we have observed in other oversea countries, to the disadvantage of Europe. Forty years ago Canada's urban population amounted to only 14 per cent of the total, but in 1921 it was more than 49 per cent.

In Sweden at the same time the urban population, and that of densely populated districts, amounted to 45 per cent of the total. We find therefore that the rush to the towns in Canada had surprisingly enough proceeded even farther than in Sweden, and just as in the U.S.A. and Australia, one may say that in Canada also the flight from the land has become a burning question, which is exciting more and more attention and alarm.

Opportunities for work in Canada are quite one-sided, since the climate and natural resources of Canada, apart from agriculture, favour a few great export industries such as lumber, pulp and paper. These are concentrated, owing to geographical conditions, in the eastern states and in British Columbia in the west, whilst agriculture occupies the three intermediate provinces of Manitoba, Saskatchewan, and Alberta. Of Canada's wheat crop in 1921 not less than 93 per cent came from the prairie provinces. Wheat production is cultivated extensively, and the whole of agriculture is conducted on the so-called "one-line farming" principle. Mixed farming, comprising all sorts of agriculture, cattle raising, etc., has reached its highest development in the eastern states. The one-sided agricultural development of the prairie provinces has, however, had unfortunate effects on the conditions of life among the rural population, in so far as it has caused violent fluctuations in the labour market. Where mixed farming has been introduced there is employment on the farms in winter also, at any rate for those who own their own land. But in the prairie provinces it is different. When the harvest has been threshed in the late autumn there is no more work to be done on the farms until the spring sowing. From 1st December to 1st April is a dead season, in which hired labour is obliged to earn a living in the forests. It is estimated that the wheat farmers require an additional supply of labour during the harvest of about 45,000 men.

A very important question in Canada is the extent to which free land is available for colonization. Before the war about 135,000 square kilometres were disposed of for colonization purposes in western Canada. In the same states there are said to remain 105,000 square kilometres of free land, but this land is in most cases at a distance of 35–40 kilometres from the railways, and its profit-earning capacity is therefore often doubtful.

Bagge sums up the situation in general in the following manner:

In Canada there is a constant demand for capable labour experienced in land work. But work cannot be guaranteed all the year round except to those who are accustomed to severe forest work or other heavy winter work. Free homesteads are only available in remote districts. Land may be purchased outright to a considerable extent, but for that purpose not inconsiderable private capital is required.

Canada would seem therefore, for Scandinavians, not to be a satisfactory substitute as an emigration country for the lost possibilities of the U.S.A., and the emigrant has only a prospect of success if he is willing to submit to the hard and exacting conditions of a settler's life. To this must be added another circumstance of great importance, and that is that Canada lacks the attraction for Scandinavian emigrants offered by the U.S.A. of an already existing considerable Scandinavian population, which gives to the emigrant the feeling that he is entering into a sympathetic circle of acquaintances or of persons with temperamental affinities.

In Canada there is, as we have already seen, a population of about 70,000 persons of Swedish origin, but this is an insignificant number compared with the 2 million persons of Swedish origin who have settled in the United States. In this connection there is an aspect of the problem which should be of special interest to English and American readers, in so far as it affords an insight into the conditions which are necessary to successful emigration from the Scandinavian countries. At the same time it contributes to our knowledge of the psychology of emigration by showing that a race may exercise a strong attraction upon its own people, even across the ocean. A Swedish settler who is successful attracts other settlers, and in this manner the volume of emigration increases automatically, when once the stream has begun to flow. Some illuminating statistics on this point may be given here.

During the year 1924 the Swedish Home Office prepared a report on those Swedish emigrants to the United States who travelled by the Swedish-American line. The investigation took place during the budget year 1st July 1922–30th June 1923, and it appears from it that the Swedish emigrants to the U.S.A. consisted for the most part of persons who already possessed near relations across the water and who therefore had been assured of work before their departure. It appears that the number of emigrants going out to relations constituted not less than two-thirds of the total, whereas about a fourth had been assisted by passage money or equipment by relatives or others. In some cases the tickets were paid for by persons resident in the U.S.A.[1] We must also consider that the larger scale of living in the U.S.A. is more stimulating to the imagination of Swedish youth, in the same way as it proves alluring to the Canadian youth.

This is one side of the problem, but on the other hand we must not forget that Canada in some respects offers greater advantages and more liberal conditions than the U.S.A. During the years

[1] "Sociala Meddelanden," No. 3, 1924, pp. 168–71.

immediately preceding the war the Canadian Government introduced certain restrictions, e.g. that it would not permit the establishment of block settlements of foreign settlers. The desired object was to disperse the various nationalities as much as possible in order more quickly to assimilate the incoming population. But this policy has now been abandoned, and the Canadian Government goes so far as to say that it was due to a misunderstanding. In any case it is now permissible to form group colonies of foreign nationalities. Finally, it must be said that conditions have materially improved since Bagge wrote his report. Times are improving, and according to information received from the employment bureau of the Swedish-American line in Winnipeg there are good openings, especially for those with a knowledge of farming and forestry. The Swedish bureau also reports that it is able to guarantee work all the year round.

The above account may suffice to give an idea of the opportunities for work offered to the emigrant to Canada, and it also affords a picture of the difficulties which the settler will encounter. It appears from the Report that Canada is a country which under present conditions is very suitable for the type of emigrant who formerly emigrated to the United States, but there are certain difficulties in creating an emigration movement. This applies also to other than the Scandinavian countries. Experience has shown that the difficulties are great in the case of British settlers also, though for reasons differing from those which restrained the Scandinavian peoples.

After the Great War efforts were made in England to encourage emigration to Canada, and up to the end of 1924 about 30,000 ex-soldiers were placed there, for which purpose the Canadian Government advanced about 100 million dollars for the promotion of emigration. This first effort in colonization was so successful that as early as 24th March 1924 almost 20 million dollars had been repaid. Subsequently the British Government made a new agreement with the Canadian Government, in accordance with the Empire Settlement Act, to receive 3,000 British families, and a loan, not exceeding £300, was made to each family. Already at this point difficulties arose, in so far as all these families have not even now been placed. A restraining influence was exercised by the bad times which supervened in Canada as elsewhere in the years after the termination of the war. A further agreement has been entered into to the effect that an additional 14,000 persons should be accepted by Canada on condition that at least half of them be trained agricultural workers. In this provision lies the chief obstacle to successful emigration from Europe, since no country can spare its agricultural workers. The European emigrants are also strongly opposed to life on the land, and prefer to find an opening in the towns. This preference is due partly to the fact that they are accustomed to town life and its distractions, and also to the circumstance that in Great Britain as in most European countries there is a surplus of manual labour or more or less trained industrial workers, but no surplus of agricultural workers, owing to the depopulation of the rural districts in favour of the towns.

It may be said, however, that Canada is a country which also offers great industrial opportunities. The development of industry during the war was considerable, though it is by no means certain that the development will continue at the same pace. Conditions are very favourable, however, for future industrial developments, perhaps chiefly on account of the numerous coalfields to be found in Canada.

"The American coalfields," writes Professor Helge Nelson, "cover a vast area. Within the United States they cover a surface of 800,000 square kilometres, and in Canada at least one-tenth as much. In other words, an area double that of Sweden contains more or less workable coal seams. The coal is found both on the plains and on the Cordillera and the Appalachians. It is only in the great Canadian primary rock that no considerable quantity of coal is present. Beyond doubt North America is the continent richest in coal. However doubtful all such estimates may be, it yet appeared from the exhaustive calculations of the Geological Congress in Canada in 1913 that the United States and Canada are the countries richest in coal, if all probable and possible resources are added to those already known. Estimates for the United States amounted to 3,900 milliard tons, and for Canada 1,200 milliard tons, whilst China appeared as a good third with 1,000 milliards, Germany with 400 milliards,[1] and Great Britain with 190 milliards. Thus almost three-quarters of the world's coal resources are to be found in North America, though it should be noted that one of the most valuable kinds of coal and the one with the greatest heating value, anthracite, is found in the largest volume in China, and even Europe possesses more than North America.

Almost all these rich coalfields are found in Alberta and British Columbia. In the latter state one also finds coal deposits passing over to anthracite by the mountain formation, both in the steep mountains and in the interior plateaus of the coastal mountain ranges. There are various natural reasons why these rich coal resources have been so little exploited hitherto. The fact that they lie almost entirely in the western parts of Canada renders them practically inaccessible to the south-eastern states, in which industrial development has hitherto been most marked.

At present the coal is used to some extent for export, but mainly for domestic use and for conversion to coke for copper smelting in British Columbia. Its use for other metallurgical industries is comparatively insignificant. Rich iron-ore deposits are found in several places, especially in the coastal districts of British Columbia, but they have not yet been worked. The minerals which are mined are nickel, copper, lead, zinc, and asbestos,

[1] 240 milliards after the war.

which are partly worked up. The tardiness of industrial development is due, however, to the fact that coal-mining in Canada in the last fifteen years has been practically stationary. In 1910 the output amounted to 12,797,000 tons, and in 1925 to no more than 13,022,000 tons, which is for all practical purposes the same quantity.[1]

Increased coal-mining presupposes either developed industries on the spot or sufficient facilities for export. Hitherto it has only been worth while to export coal from the central districts, for example, from Vancouver. It is therefore of great importance to Canada to increase the value of its coal by refining processes, in order that it may command a higher price and transport costs be of comparatively less importance. If it is true that the Germans have succeeded by the Bergius process in extracting petroleum from coal in the proportion of one ton of oil from three tons of coal, at a price which can compete with natural oil, there should be great possibilities for the development of Canadian coal-mining.

British Columbia also possesses other power resources, in so far as all the important rivers running into the Pacific Ocean, with the exception of the Colorado river, have their source in that state. It is reported that in 1923, 300,000 electric h.p. were developed and consumed by industry,

[1] "Encyclopædia Britannica," Suppl. Volumes, 13th Edit., Vol. 1, p. 507.

by the towns and by agriculture. About 40,000 h.p. were developed for sawmills, pulp factories and paper mills, and 30,000 for mining and metallurgical industry. According to an estimate of the Dominion Government the water power of British Columbia is capable of developing 3,000,000 h.p., which is the equivalent of the enormous figure of nearly 20 milliard kw. per annum.[1] It may also be mentioned that Canada is reputed to possess rich oilfields, though they are so situated that difficulties of transport at present prevent their exploitation.

In addition to other rich natural resources, Canada also possesses vast forests. The area of sawn goods timber is estimated at 246 million acres at the least, of which British Columbia alone has 50 million acres.[2] It may be added that the finest forests are reputed to be in British Columbia. The remarkable thing is that in British Columbia new growth makes good the losses by felling, fire, or other causes. This is not due to the existence of any scientific forestry, but rather to the fact that the damp and mild climate of the Pacific Coast stimulates a regrowth which is estimated as twice as great as the average regrowth in the rest of Canada.[3]

[1] Hans Bergman: "British Columbia: Swedish Settlers," Victoria, B.C., 1923, p. 121.

[2] Raphael Zon and W. M. Sparhawk: "Forest Resources of the World," McGraw Hill Book Co. Inc., New York, 1923, Vol. 2, p. 498.

[3] *Ibidem*, p. 504.

British Columbia offers in many respects most favourable conditions to European emigrants, especially as the climatic conditions are very good. In the prairie provinces the winters are very severe, but already in Alberta they are tempered by winds from the Pacific, and in British Columbia the climate may be characterized as extremely healthy, not only for North Europeans, but also for most of the races inhabiting the temperate zones.

The climate has many resemblances to that of European countries in the same latitude. On the coasts the winter is mild and the summer cool. The rainfall is copious, especially along the coast. In the interior, where the rainfall is not sufficient, there is access to the great rivers and the abundant water reservoirs in the mountains, so that there is a possibility of cheap artificial irrigation.

The country is suitable for all kinds of agriculture. On the high plateaus cattle can graze, and the soil is suitable, according to altitude and geographical position, not only for the cultivation of grain, but also for fruit and vegetables, including practically every imaginable fruit, from the southern grape to all the fruits of temperate climes such as apples, pears, raspberries, gooseberries, strawberries, etc. Dairy farming and feather farming are prosperous and have great opportunities for further development. In other words, British Columbia is the place for agricultural specialists of all kinds.

Each may cultivate his own special interests, which in its turn must react favourably on a considerable colonization. Finally it may be pointed out that there are here vast areas which can be opened up by the surplus population of Europe. British Columbia from north to south is 700 English miles long and 400 miles broad from east to west. It is situated between the 49th degree of latitude in the south and 60th degree in the north, and has an area of about 353,000 square miles. It is therefore greater in extent than the three Scandinavian countries put together, and has an area almost three times as great as that of Great Britain and Ireland.

CHAPTER XIII

THE WHITE MAN IN THE TROPICS

The Problem of Cool Rooms

AN important aspect of the colonization problem is the question whether unexploited districts are suitable for settlement by the white races. Opinions in this matter may be divided, but so much is certain, that great districts still exist in Australia and Africa, in parts of the high plateaus of Latin America, i.e. in Mexico and the South American states, which are well adapted to such exploitation. In addition there are plains and other territory in the southern parts of the Argentine, and perhaps also in Chile. The possibility of employing white men is also bound up with the question what sort of labour is required. European agricultural labour, miners and industrial workers cannot be unreservedly advised to settle in the tropics except in districts climatically suitable, where their employment has been previously organized and financed. But there is no reason why expert labour, such as that of engineers, foresters, doctors and more or less scientifically trained persons, should not settle almost anywhere in the tropics with good prospects of success.

It is possible, moreover, that the obstacles to white colonization of the tropical zones may be overcome by engineering skill and the progress of medical science. Many people will perhaps think this view too optimistic, but I cannot help thinking that the President of the German Reichsbank is quite right when he says in his address on the "New Colonial Policy" that:

"Pessimists immediately object that it is impossible for the white man to live in the tropics. They make this objection for the same reason as do all unenterprising people when called upon to try something new. They prefer to do nothing at all. The objection is also based on the fact that most individuals think only in years or decades, whereas it is man's duty to think in generations. He who feels himself a conscious link in the chain of human development must easily perceive that to the emigrants who once sailed in the 'Mayflower' to America its forests were not less terrifying and its experiences not less strenuous than those which the still unexplored territories of the earth may be expected to present to the modern emigrant.

"We must also consider," he continues, "that scientific research and engineering science have very greatly facilitated colonization. Motors, flying machines, wireless telegraphy and telephony are modern auxiliaries which offer possibilities, unknown to our forefathers, of overcoming the difficulties of the still virgin territories of the earth. Medical science has also made it possible in the domain of hygiene to subdue the contagious tropical diseases in a manner quite unknown to former times. Modern man therefore possesses the means of exploiting colonial areas which our forefathers, without their assistance, could not turn to advantage."

One part of the earth which has hitherto been regarded as impenetrable to white men for purposes of exploitation, owing to the murderous climatic conditions, is the vast district of the river Amazon. Recently, however, two American scientific expeditions have explored and surveyed this district and have come, at least partially, to a more favourable conclusion. The one was the so-called Alexander Hamilton-Rice expedition, which surveyed the district in a hydroplane to an extent of about 12,000 miles.[1] It started in 1924 and stayed out for about a year. The expedition came to the conclusion that the climatic difficulties were not insurmountable. According to their report the most dangerous zone is the lower course of the river, but as soon as one comes higher up in the hilly districts there is no longer any need to be afraid of fevers. If anybody is smitten with a tropical fever it is due to accidental causes such as chill, etc.

Somewhat later another American expedition, consisting of six experts, dispatched by the United States Department of Commerce, set out for the same and neighbouring districts. During ten months the expedition explored in its own vessel 37 different

[1] "The National Geographic Magazine," April 1926, pp. 353 *et seqq.*

rivers, all belonging to the Amazon system, for a combined distance of nearly 20,000 miles.[1] The final conclusion as regards the climate was that apart from certain districts, which are very ill-favoured either as a result of human neglect or by bad natural conditions, the climate is not unhealthy. The white man can very well live there and preserve excellent health, but it must be noticed that he will pay dearly for the neglect if he does not observe the elementary rules of hygiene. Malaria in a more or less severe form ravages certain districts, but in wide areas the disease does not exist at all.

The Brazilian Government has done very little as yet to introduce sound conditions, but the awakening interest of other nations in these districts has stimulated the Brazilian Government also. It has therefore recently taken the initiative in order to promote colonization there. Thus, for example, there is at present under discussion a proposal to grant a large concession in the Amazon district to Japanese settlers. It is supposed that it ought to be possible to acclimatize there a subtropical people like the Japanese. It is reported that some enterprising individuals are examining the question, and if the investigations now in progress are satisfactory, it is probable that Japanese colonization will take place. The Japanese Kanega

[1] "The National Geographic Magazine," April 1926, p. 465 *et seq.*

Fuchi spinning company has made a grant of 80,000 yen in order to send out a commission of inquiry to the proposed district.

Another question is to what extent Europeans can acclimatize themselves in the Amazon district and other similar tropical areas. Hitherto it has been taken for granted that the white man is not suited for the colonization of tropical countries. The problem is much more simple when it is only a question of the occupation by white men of the numerous tropical plateaus, but even this problem cannot be said to have been finally solved.

"Although Europeans have been engaged for the past 300 years in economic enterprises in the tropics," writes one of the greatest modern experts in tropical culture, the former Governor of German New Guinea, Geheimrat Dr. Hahl,[1] "yet the problem of settlement in the tropical highlands is not yet solved. The reason is not far to seek. The colonial empires which have a surplus population, such as Russia and England, have at their disposal large areas in the temperate zones, and even to-day they possess millions of hectares of fertile land and they therefore have no need to lay claim to the tropical highlands. If we look at the Latin colonizing Powers, neither France, Spain nor Portugal has for a long time past had any surplus population to compel them seriously to concern themselves with questions of emigration and settlement overseas. The few Italian colonies possess no highlands suitable for colonization. Italian emigration has therefore been directed to foreign lands within the temperate zones. Similarly the surplus population of the Scandinavian countries, the Russian border states, Austria-Hungary, and finally Ger-

[1] "Die Ansiedelung von Europäern in den Tropen," Koloniale Rundschau, Heft 4, 1920, pp. 174–5.

many, has emigrated to the temperate zones. The emigrants from states possessing no colonies went mainly to North America. Yet Europeans have not altogether avoided the tropical highlands. It may therefore be useful to examine the experience they have had there up to the present.

" Among the Little Antilles is situated the island of Saba, belonging to the Dutch, with an area of about 12 square kilometres. This island rises steeply out of the sea to a height of about 2,500 feet. Under its favourable climate Europeans, of Scandinavian and English origin, have been permanently settled on this island for upwards of 200 years,[1] and in Central America it may be regarded as proved that white settlers with their families thrive at a height of over 3,000 feet.

" European settlers have thriven best," he continues, " in the Mexican highlands, even though there are no results of experiments on a large scale and for a longer period. Unstable political conditions and transport difficulties still make emigration to Mexico undesirable. The German settlers in the Brazilian state of Espirito Santo have dwelt there for three generations and have shown a great increase."

The problem of future white colonization in the tropics, whether in the highlands or lowlands, is, as Dr. Schacht says, quite different from what it was, since modern science and engineering have discovered a number of improvements which may assist in overcoming climatic difficulties. Among them must be included modern refrigerating technique, if only its attention could be directed into this field.

An eminent Swede, who has lived for a long time

[1] The Scandinavians consist mainly of Swedish and Danish emigrants, but they have forgotten their mother tongue and speak English.

in the tropics, and especially in Sumatra, partly employed as an expert under the Dutch Government and partly as head of a large experimental station, Dr. Björn Palm, now Swedish Consul-General in Guatemala, states, in a report which he has shown to the writer, that he regards a white colonization of the tropics as practicable, assuming that the present obstacles of a more or less technical kind are either neutralized or entirely removed. The use of the white man's labour in the tropics is hindered, he says, partly by the physical exhaustion resulting from the high temperature, and partly from the purely psychological burden which accompanies the necessity of working under such conditions. The exact opposite picture of colonization under extreme climatic conditions is afforded in the northern latitudes of Sweden. For timber cutting or mining in Norrland a regulation of the temperature is necessary during rest periods or during work. If it is cold out of doors it must be warm indoors. The contrary is true of the tropics. If it is hot outside it must be cool inside. If, therefore, the tropical conditions could be regulated in this respect in accordance with the requirements of the human organism a profound influence would be brought to bear on the possibilities of colonization. If the colonist after a day's work in the tropical heat could retire into a home of normal temperature and normal humidity, a real revolution in living conditions in the tropics would thereby be accomplished. It is conceivable that modern refrigerating science may solve this problem.

At present there are on the market several refrigerating apparatuses, such as the Frigidaire of the General Motors, the Kelvinator, the Electrolux, and others, but these have for the present only been tried out for ice safes. But modern refrigerators would acquire a new significance if they could be adapted for the cooling of workshops or dwelling-houses in tropical countries.

Dr. Palm rightly considers it most curious that no practical experiments whatever have been made in regulating the temperature in tropical dwellings. The architects and builders there remain, he says, on the same level as regards regulation of the temperature of dwellings as were the mediæval builders in Europe. In northern latitudes heating technique has been adopted, in proportion as it has improved, in order to regulate indoor temperature, but conditions in the tropics remain as primitive as of old. To exclude the heat and damp from dwellings nothing has been done beyond the use of more or less insulating building materials. In order to lower the temperature scarcely any other method has been employed than the use of ice and the endeavour to secure change of air by means of draughts or fans. So far as we know, there has been no attempt to obtain a suitable temperature by artificial cooling.

Apart from the general significance of temperate rooms, Dr. Palm points to a couple of special cases in which the adoption of refrigerating technique would be of great importance. Tropical hotel rooms are among the least agreeable experiences of a prolonged stay in the tropics. Cool hotel rooms would be an immense comfort to travellers and would doubtless also be profitable to their proprietors. Despite ventilation, railway and steamship journeys in tropical countries are as a rule not alluring. Cooled cabins and railway compartments, on the other hand, would be in every way stimulating.

The problem is to what extent, with the aid of modern refrigerating technique, an apparatus could be constructed which, at least assuming proper insulation, would accomplish a sufficient reduction of temperature and at the same time effect a considerable reduction in the humidity of the atmosphere. In a tropical climate damp is just as unpleasant as heat, and the problem is therefore twofold. It is just as important to reduce the temperature as to reduce the humidity to the desired extent. Very few, if any, practical attempts have been made in this direction, in any case none of commercial importance. On the other hand, it is known that in German submarines and on vessels stationed in the tropics experiments have been made to produce cool air of suitable humidity for a limited period of say six hours in the hermetically sealed bridge cabin from which the battle is directed. It is reported that the problem in this case was solved, but probably the process is very expensive. For a practical solution of the problem it is necessary in the first instance to determine what it is desired to achieve.

The human body constantly seeks, says a German report, to adapt itself to the temperature of the surrounding atmosphere in order to maintain the normal blood temperature (37° Centigrade) constant. For that reason perspiration occurs with an increased temperature in the air in which we happen to be. By the evaporation of the perspiration the temperature of the skin is lowered and thereby that of the whole body. The possibility of perspiring is dependent on the relative humidity of the surrounding atmosphere not exceeding 98 per cent, and further on its temperature not exceeding that of the human body, or 37° Centigrade. If the humidity of the surrounding atmosphere exceeds 98 per cent then the perspiration cannot be absorbed by it by evaporation, since the air has taken up all the moisture it is capable of absorbing. Neither can the temperature of the body be regulated by giving off heat into the surrounding atmosphere, because at 37° the latter corresponds to the temperature of the human blood. The consequence is that the fine pores of the human skin are sealed by the perspiration, which cannot be thrown off into the already saturated atmosphere. Consequently this condition gradually leads to a heat-stroke.

In this connection it may also be noted that the experts in hygiene particularly emphasize the fact that one of the most important conditions of successfully exposing the human body to damp and heat is to keep the air in circulation. If this is done, much of the discomfort disappears owing to the fact that perspiration is promoted. Modern refrigerators reduce the temperature and fix the water vapour in the form of ice. It would seem that such a modern refrigerator should be combined with a fan in order to set the air in motion. As it is possible that the refrigerating process would not remove sufficient water, some chemical means should be adopted to absorb enough moisture to leave the cooled air sufficiently dry. The problem is simplified by the fact that cold air is heavier than hot air. If the refrigerator were placed in the ceiling the cold dry air would sink down into the room and would fill it and replace the hot air sucked up by the fans. How high the percentage of humidity should be at various temperatures is a matter which hygienists must determine experimentally. The problem is, as we have seen, very complicated, but perhaps not so difficult that we may not see a solution in the not too distant future.

CHAPTER XIV

THE CREATION OF NEW VALUES

World Economy, Enterprise and New Invention

IN an article entitled "The Economic Factor in Contemporary Politics,"[1] Maurice Caudel develops views which throw a new light on the connection between economics and politics in our time. His conclusion is that the economic factor is the sole determining one and that politics are passing through a period of decadence which has assumed such a menacing form that it may involve danger to the future existence of European civilization.

The problem of world economics has changed greatly in the last hundred years. Everybody must see that it is quite a different thing to feed 1,800 million mouths as compared with the former necessity of feeding only about a third of that number. At the same time the material needs of mankind have increased far beyond the need for

[1] Maurice Caudel: "Le rôle du facteur économique dans la politique contemporaine," "Revue économique internationale," Goemaere, Bruxelles, May 1926, p. 213.

daily bread, and these needs begin to manifest themselves also among primitive races, in so far as even backward peoples, who may themselves be bad producers, eagerly purchase, as far as they can, the products of modern industry.

These increased needs have been accompanied by one advantage: that man has been compelled to work harder. He exerts himself often to the utmost, perhaps principally in order to satisfy his material desires.

"Mankind," to quote Caudel again, "is more active than ever and seeks to displace the manual labour of other ages by a methodical, carefully calculated, intensive, but also more mechanical labour."

Instead of tilling the soil individually as in former times, or carrying on a sound trade as a craftsman, man has developed large-scale enterprises with combined activity in immense factories, and he bases his manufacture on mechanical inventions. This quality of combination in modern enterprise is, according to Caudel, the most characteristic feature of modern man and gives him a special position in the world's history. Modern man is constantly striving to discover something new and is becoming more and more an imaginative being in his economic activity. Sometimes ideas fail him, but he always exerts himself to find new ones and spends much time and energy in developing them.

In reality there are only a few men, principally learned men, who study and combine to find the new idea, but the learned and the inventive are not usually in a position to exploit their ideas, but must seek the help of the manufacturer or the organizing genius, who exercises his imagination in its practical execution. His creative faculty must therefore have a practical side, so that he may see how to utilize the possibilities of an idea in the most profitable manner. He is the head, who understands, takes risks, directs, and therefore plays the chief rôle in modern life. When he realizes that a solution of the economic problem is impossible within the bounds of Europe, he turns his glance abroad. The surplus population which oppresses Europe must be transferred to those quarters of the globe where there exist unexploited natural resources worth developing by present-day technical methods. Thus there arises, and must arise according to Caudel, besides the modern industrial pioneer, the colonizing pioneer, who must avail himself of the spirit of enterprise of which we in our day are in such crying need. Raw materials and foodstuffs must be acquired, but at the same time it is probable that we shall no longer be able to continue to produce in Europe to the same extent as at present all the goods which may in the future be more cheaply and more naturally produced in oversea countries.

The economic factor tends to predominate everywhere in modern developments and the future lies with the pioneer. The masses, lacking creative imagination, remain passive, but follow him in order to participate in his profits. Those who cannot do so are discontented, but necessity knows no law, and they are left behind. It is only exceptional talent which reaps a reward, and not least in the physical sphere. We may point to the large prizes which are distributed in all sorts of sports competitions. But it is not usually profitable to be a politician or to work in theory for science or for social ideals. Very few are the gifted men who seriously devote themselves to politics. Yet the great decline in interest in political life is in many respects to be deplored and it reveals dangerous conflicts in modern social life. The citizen turns away from politics, but at the same time demands that the organized forces of society should automatically guarantee order and security. The equality which was the dream of the French Revolution, and later of Socialism, is quite old-fashioned. The one who succeeds in modern society is rather, I would prefer to say, what Nietzsche called the "happy exception," the one who is hard enough, and has the will to power. But at the same time the framework of society has crumpled. There is no longer any particular class which is favoured, but it is the arrivist, whoever he may be, who is successful and forces his way to a dominating position.

The economic factor is the most active element in the process of fermentation which mankind calls progress. This factor comprises in itself everything, good and bad, to be found in man. It stimulates his ambitions, but makes him less careful of the means of attaining it. The chief thing is to succeed, morals take a second place. Only those who fail are ethically condemned. All this selfish striving renders the maintenance of the modern state more difficult, in so far as there is required of politics a solution of the essentially insoluble problem of creating meticulous regulations, just laws, and stable institutions in a world which under the pressure of the economic spur is in a state of constant flux.

The difficulties of the situation may be studied, among other things, in the tariff legislation of the various modern states. The desired object is to devise a tariff under which domestic industry can work most profitably. The ideal would therefore be a strictly scientific customs tariff, but the fact is that as yet nobody has succeeded in constructing one. The American customs tariff of 1921 contains an elastic clause according to which the President has the right to raise or lower a duty by 50 per cent. A special tariff commission is appointed to discover the difference between the costs of production of a certain article in the U.S.A. and the costs of production of the same article in other countries, in order to regulate the tariff accordingly. Two years after the law was passed the commission had only concluded its investigations in the case of three articles, of which two were in very limited use, sodium nitrate and barium oxide. On the third, such an important article as wheat, the commission was quite unable to agree or to offer any acceptable calculation. The reason of this failure is that every economic factor is extremely complex. Values can only be established, as it were, for a moment. They constantly change, because they are the result of constantly fluctuating, and very shifting, factors. "These factors arise," writes Caudel, "from the incessant variations which are caused by the increasing economic war between men, between peoples, and between individuals, a war which never knows any conclusion of peace." But the well-being of the nations no longer depends on natural advantages and commercial activity alone. There has been added an element of surprise in the form of inventions and discoveries, which may in a turn of the hand alter the whole world situation in respect of a particular article.

It is this which makes modern developments so uncertain, since at any moment we may be confronted by an unforeseen situation, and he who to-day holds the trump card may be surprised to see the game suddenly taken out of his hands.

Great Britain better than any other country affords an example of the strength of historical development. By centuries of consistent effort it has understood how to control world trade. But in our days this supremacy is threatened by the U.S.A., and we can see that Great Britain only holds her own with the greatest difficulty. It has therefore with good reason been remarked how important it is for any Englishman to remember the words of Cecil Rhodes:

> "Every schoolmaster in England should once every year remind his pupils that England does not consist merely of the British Isles, but of the whole world, in the sense that England's power consists in holding open all the markets of the world. England is only a spot on the globe, but it will remain the first Great Power so long as it commands its present markets."

England must consistently maintain the commercial policy advocated by Cecil Rhodes in order to preserve its position. But to practise free trade and effect low costs of production in a materialistic society in which everybody cries out for quick profits is difficult. Parliamentarism and democratic influence also make claims upon the State which are not consistent with economy, and may sometimes be very dangerous. We have seen during the summer of 1925 how the miners' threat of a strike forced the British Government to grant large subsidies, not less than £23 millions, to the coal industry in order to get coal which it was not profitable to get at the wages then paid. This concession could of course only be made at the expense of other classes of society. The miners' leaders no doubt imagined that they were promoting social progress, but in reality they did just the contrary. The subsidy was a retrograde step in England's economics, because it laid hands on part of the diminished resources which England still had at its disposal. The English coal strike and the subsequent General Strike have shown even more clearly how fatefully social politics may affect modern society. The result has been that the national income is not sufficient. Even wealthy Great Britain may soon be compelled to live on its capital.

The remedy for all the complications arising from the immense indebtedness of the nations and from the impoverishing effects of the world war, the extensive social experiments called forth by them, etc., can only be found in inventions and in the pioneer activity capable of exploiting new ideas of world-wide economic importance. But even inventions and pioneer activity have their other side. We must remember especially that they not only create new values but also destroy old ones, which we had perhaps imagined to be constant. Countries which were formerly rich owing to their resources in raw materials may become poor whilst still retaining those resources, and states which do not possess them may, conversely, owing to successful inventions and far-sighted pioneer activity acquire wealth at the cost of the former. A couple of examples may suffice. In another connection we have already pointed out the significance of the fact that coal no longer occupies the same leading position as formerly as fuel for the production of power. One of the principal causes of the economic difficulties of Great Britain is, as is well known, that oil has begun to supplant coal so widely for power purposes, e.g. in ships. Similarly the use of hydro-electric power has become much more general, especially in countries which lack coal. Such countries therefore now import less.

Another striking example of the fallen value of a raw material consequent upon new methods and new discoveries is afforded by the production of raw rubber. Even as late as the close of the last century Brazil was the country which supplied the whole world with raw rubber from its forests. Nowadays Brazil only produces 5 per cent of the world's production, whilst British and Dutch Indies rubber plantations provide the remaining 95 per cent. The enterprise which created this development operates with a capital of about £150 millions. Its success is the result of twenty-five years of strenuous effort. But should the synthetic production of rubber ever be achieved we may perhaps witness a similar world crisis in this raw material.

In spite of the disadvantages and difficulties which accompany modern inventions and modern enterprise, yet the latter would seem to constitute the only means by which the civilized races can possibly escape from the present economic confusion. Political democracy has shown itself, both internationally in the Versailles treaty and in the social and political developments of the various countries, completely incapable of opening up new avenues to a prosperous future.

The President of the German Reichsbank, Dr. Schacht, comes to the same conclusion in his address on the new colonial policy. The Dawes plan has had the advantage that it has pointed to capitalism as the only way of escape from the present chaos. The world war has shown the impossibility of one-sided Imperialism, and the Russian misery has clearly revealed the false assumptions of Socialism and Communism.

" The individualistic, capitalistic, economic order is the only saviour visible," writes Schacht, " and capitalism is the only form of human enterprise which presupposes a strong sense of moral responsibility."

If one glances back a century, and makes a comparison between conditions now and after the Napoleonic wars, the present situation must be regarded as an advance in so far as the modern spirit of enterprise has considerably widened our horizon. At the end of the eighteenth century, and the beginning of the nineteenth, the so-called physiocratic theory prevailed in economic questions, and had its chief significance in its opposition to, and criticism of, the earlier prevalent mercantile theory. But the physiocrats in their turn had also a somewhat narrow conception of economic laws and laid an undue emphasis on agriculture, which they regarded as the only productive occupation.

"Neither industry nor commerce can add to the world's wealth," they say, "for the product of either of these branches has never, under actual conditions, a higher value than the quantity of agricultural produce which in the form of raw materials, implements, maintenance of labour, and profit on capital which has gone to the making of that product."

The great significance of the physiocratic system is to be found in the fact that it directed attention from narrow national points of view to international conceptions. This became even clearer among the successors of the physiocrats and especially in Adam Smith, who in his classic work the "Wealth of Nations" freed himself from the one-sided physiocratic emphasis on the importance of agriculture and had a certain understanding of the possibility of creating new values in a different way.

His book appeared in 1776, just at the dawn of the industrial revolution, at the time, for example, when Watt discovered the use of steam as a motive power. But Adam Smith describes a capitalistic enterprise which was still in its infancy, and he scarcely imagined how great were the changes to come.

It was reserved for the nineteenth century, by means of a combination of inventive genius and industrial and commercial activity to create the new foundation of human development. The necessity of progress on the same lines has become even more acute since the Great War, and it is only now that the pioneer type described by Caudel emerges as a fully developed personality.

If one goes back to the novelists of the first half of the nineteenth century, and especially to the greatest painter of humanity of his day, Honoré Balzac, who occupied himself more than any other writer with character drawing and descriptions of the business life of his day, the great difference between then and now appears in the most vivid colours. One may say of all his characters that they lack vision. Financiers, stockbrokers, perfumiers, or whatever they may be, have only one motive to action—a most narrow-minded greed of gain. Balzac's leading spirits can only think of the amassing of wealth at the cost of others.

In other words, he had no comprehension of the importance of modern industry and commerce, but was more or less captive to the economic outlook of the physiocrats: "One can only get rich by the ruin of others." The reason is that the idea of capital, in the sense that mankind can acquire new wealth by economic enterprise, had not yet dawned on the general consciousness.

Balzac's importance as the painter of his own times, or as he himself expresses it, as its natural scientist, has from this point of view certainly been too little appreciated by literary critics. They have mostly plunged into æsthetic valuations and descriptions of certain characters. They have concerned themselves less with the picture of society as a whole which Balzac endeavoured to present from as many points of view as possible. If, for example, one turns to Georg Brandes' "Main Currents of Nineteenth Century Literature," we find there exhaustive comment on Balzac's treatment of such types as the young snob Rastignac, and some of his female characters pass in review. Brandes also describes Balzac's genius for giving a living picture of Paris itself and its teeming life, but there is lacking, on the other hand, any appreciation of the rich gallery of middle-class business men, and *nouveaux riches* of the day, which one finds in such abundance in Balzac's novels. Who does not remember Baron de Nucingen, the representative of the philistine *haute finance* of the day, the upstart and ambitious F. de Tillet, and all the typical characters, right down to the usurer, the Dutchman and the half Jew Van Gobseck, banker in the same way as an executioner is a surgeon.[1]

From the point of view of present-day perception of the historical and literary relationship it must be admitted that it is the descriptions of the business atmosphere and its complications in Balzac which constitute the most interesting pages in his works. It is just by these descriptions and accounts of the economic life, its organization and significance, in the Paris of his day that Balzac has made his most important contribution to the history of civilization. By his brilliant descriptions of this kind he has also become an inexhaustible source of our knowledge

[1] "Œuvres Complètes d'Honoré de Balzac," Tome II, César Birottean Louis Conard, Paris, 1918, p. 25.

of the outlook of that age on economic and social problems, and its opinions upon them.

The type of modern enterprise, as Caudel writes, has perhaps not yet found its poet, but we nevertheless often find him foreshadowed in literature, as for example in Nietzsche, as a superman, who because he can create something new, claims the right to set himself above ordinary morals and to stand outside the limits of the permissible. The tragic significance of this figure has moreover already been described by Ibsen in Johan Gabriel Borkman, the man who knew he had to create something new, which would bring bread to thousands of mouths, but who fell because his fellow-men did not understand him and would not allow him to take the risks which he thought himself entitled to take.

The progress which has been made during the last century may be summed up by saying that mankind nowadays really believes in a new birth, and if this faith can be maintained we need not be apprehensive for the future of the West.

INDEX

INDEX

METHUEN'S GENERAL LITERATURE

A SELECTION OF

MESSRS. METHUEN'S PUBLICATIONS

This Catalogue contains only a selection of the more important books published by Messrs. Methuen. A complete catalogue of their publications may be obtained on application.

PART I. GENERAL LITERATURE

Allen (R. Wilberforce)
METHODISM AND MODERN WORLD PROBLEMS. *Crown 8vo.* 7*s.* 6*d. net.*

Bain (F. W.)
A DIGIT OF THE MOON. THE DESCENT OF THE SUN. A HEIFER OF THE DAWN. IN THE GREAT GOD'S HAIR. A DRAUGHT OF THE BLUE. AN ESSENCE OF THE DUSK. AN INCARNATION OF THE SNOW. A MINE OF FAULTS. THE ASHES OF A GOD. BUBBLES OF THE FOAM. A SYRUP OF THE BEES. THE LIVERY OF EVE. THE SUBSTANCE OF A DREAM. *All Fcap. 8vo.* 5*s. net.* AN ECHO OF THE SPHERES. *Wide Demy 8vo.* 10*s.* 6*d. net.*

Balfour (Sir Graham)
THE LIFE OF ROBERT LOUIS STEVENSON. *Twentieth Edition. In one Volume. Cr. 8vo. Buckram,* 7*s.* 6*d. net.*

Barker (Ernest)
NATIONAL CHARACTER. *Demy 8vo.* 10*s.* 6*d. net.* GREEK POLITICAL THEORY: Plato and his Predecessors. *Second Edition. Demy 8vo.* 14*s. net.*

Belfield (Reginald)
FROM LANDSCAPE TO STUDIO. Illustrated. *Fcap. 4to.* 12*s.* 6*d. net.*

Belloc (Hilaire)
PARIS. THE PYRENEES. *Each* 8*s.* 6*d. net.* ON NOTHING. HILLS AND THE SEA. ON SOMETHING. THIS AND THAT AND THE OTHER. ON. *Each* 6*s. net.* FIRST AND LAST. ON EVERYTHING. ON ANYTHING. EMMANUEL BURDEN. *Each* 3*s.* 6*d. net.* MARIE ANTOINETTE. 18*s. net.* A HISTORY OF ENGLAND. In 5 vols. Vols. I and II. 15*s.* net each.

Birmingham (George A.)
A WAYFARER IN HUNGARY. Illustrated. 8*s.* 6*d. net.* A WAYFARER IN IRELAND. Illustrated. 7*s.* 6*d. net.* SPILLIKINS: a Book of Essays. 3*s.* 6*d. net.* SHIPS AND SEALING WAX: a Book of Essays. 5*s. net.*

Bowles (George F. S.)
THE STRENGTH OF ENGLAND. *Demy 8vo.* 8*s.* 6*d. net.*

Budge (Sir E. A. Wallis)
A HISTORY OF ETHIOPIA. Illustrated. In 2 vols. £3 3*s. net.*

Glover (T. R.)
THE CONFLICT OF RELIGIONS IN THE EARLY ROMAN EMPIRE. POETS AND PURITANS. VIRGIL. *Each* 10*s*. 6*d*. *net*. FROM PERICLES TO PHILIP. 12*s*. 6*d*. *net*.

Graham (Harry)
THE WORLD WE LAUGH IN: More Deportmental Ditties. Illustrated by "FISH." *Sixth Edition. Fcap.* 8*vo*. 5*s*. *net*. STRAINED RELATIONS. Illustrated by H. STUART MENZIES and HENDY. *Royal* 16*mo*. 6*s*. *net*.

Grahame (Kenneth)
THE WIND IN THE WILLOWS. *Nineteenth Edition. Crown* 8*vo*. 7*s*. 6*d*. *net*. Also, illustrated by WYNDHAM PAYNE. *Small* 4to. 7*s*. 6*d*. net. Also unillustrated. *Fcap*. 8*vo*. 3*s*. 6*d*. *net*.

Hadfield (J. A.)
PSYCHOLOGY AND MORALS. *Seventh Edition. Crown* 8*vo*. 6*s*. *net*.

Hall (H. R.)
THE ANCIENT HISTORY OF THE NEAR EAST. *Seventh Edition, Revised. Demy* 8*vo*. £1 1*s*. *net*. THE CIVILIZATION OF GREECE IN THE BRONZE AGE. Illustrated. *Wide Royal* 8*vo*. £1 10*s*. *net*.

Hamer (Sir W. H.), and Hutt (C. W.)
A MANUAL OF HYGIENE. Illustrated. *Demy* 8*vo*. £1 10*s*. *net*.

Hewlett (Maurice)
THE LETTERS OF MAURICE HEWLETT. Edited by LAURENCE BINYON. Illustrated. *Demy* 8*vo*. 18*s*. *net*.

Hind (A. M.)
A CATALOGUE OF REMBRANDT'S ETCHINGS. Two Vols. Profusely Illustrated. *Wide Royal* 8*vo*. £1 15*s*. *net*.

Holdsworth (W. S.)
A HISTORY OF ENGLISH LAW. Nine Volumes. *Demy* 8*vo*. £1 5*s*. *net each*.

Hudson (W. H.)
A SHEPHERD'S LIFE. Illustrated. *Demy* 8*vo*. 10*s*. 6*d*. *net*. Also, unillustrated. *Fcap*. 8*vo*. 3*s*. 6*d*. *net*.

Hutton (Edward)
CITIES OF SICILY. Illustrated. 10*s*. 6*d*. *net*. MILAN AND LOMBARDY. THE CITIES OF ROMAGNA AND THE MARCHES. SIENA AND SOUTHERN TUSCANY. VENICE AND VENETIA. THE CITIES OF SPAIN. NAPLES AND SOUTHERN ITALY. Illustrated. *Each*, 8*s*. 6*d*. *net*. A WAYFARER IN UNKNOWN TUSCANY. THE CITIES OF UMBRIA. COUNTRY WALKS ABOUT FLORENCE. ROME. FLORENCE AND NORTHERN TUSCANY. Illustrated. *Each* 7*s*. 6*d*. *net*.

Imms (A. D.)
A GENERAL TEXTBOOK OF ENTOMOLOGY. Illustrated. *Royal* 8*vo*. £1 16*s*. *net*.

Inge (W. R.), D.D., Dean of St. Paul's
CHRISTIAN MYSTICISM. (The Bampton Lectures of 1899.) *Sixth Edition. Crown* 8*vo*. 7*s*. 6*d*. *net*.

Jackson (H. C.)
OSMAN DIGNA. *Demy* 8*vo*. 12*s*. 6*d*. *net*.

Kipling (Rudyard)
BARRACK-ROOM BALLADS. 241*st Thousand*.
THE SEVEN SEAS. 180*th Thousand*.
THE FIVE NATIONS. 139*th Thousand*.
DEPARTMENTAL DITTIES. 111*th Thousand*.
THE YEARS BETWEEN. 95*th Thousand*.
Four Editions of these famous volumes of poems are now published, viz.:— *Crown* 8*vo*. *Buckram*, 7*s*. 6*d*. *net*. *Fcap*. 8vo. *Cloth*, 6*s*. *net*. *Leather*, 7*s*. 6*d*. *net*. Service Edition. Two volumes each book. *Square Fcap*. 8*vo*. 3*s*. *net* each volume.
A KIPLING ANTHOLOGY—Verse. *Fcap*. 8*vo*. *Cloth*, 6*s*. *net*. *Leather*, 7*s*. 6*d*. *net*.
TWENTY POEMS FROM RUDYARD KIPLING. 447*th Thousand*. *Fcap*. 8*vo*. 1*s*. *net*.
A CHOICE OF SONGS. *Second Edition*. *Fcap*. 8*vo*. 2*s*. *net*.

Lamb (Charles and Mary)
THE COMPLETE WORKS. Edited by E. V. LUCAS. A New and Revised Edition in Six Volumes. With Frontispieces. *Fcap*. 8*vo*. 6*s*. *net each*.
The volumes are: I. MISCELLANEOUS PROSE. II. ELIA AND THE LAST ESSAYS OF ELIA. III. BOOKS FOR CHILDREN. IV. PLAYS AND POEMS. V. and VI. LETTERS.
SELECTED LETTERS. Chosen and Edited by G. T. CLAPTON. *Fcap*. 8*vo*. 3*s*. 6*d*. *net*.
THE CHARLES LAMB DAY BOOK. Compiled by E. V. LUCAS. *Fcap*. 8*vo*. 6*s*. *net*.

Lankester (Sir Ray)
SCIENCE FROM AN EASY CHAIR. SCIENCE FROM AN EASY CHAIR: Second Series. DIVERSIONS OF A NATURALIST. GREAT AND SMALL THINGS. Illustrated. *Crown* 8*vo*. 7*s*. 6*d*. *net*. SECRETS OF EARTH AND SEA. Illustrated. *Crown* 8*vo*. 8*s*. 6*d*. *net*.

Lodge (Sir Oliver)
MAN AND THE UNIVERSE (*Twentieth Edition*). THE SURVIVAL OF MAN (*Seventh Edition*). *Each Crown* 8*vo*. 7*s*. 6*d*. *net*. RAYMOND (*Thirteenth Edition*). *Demy* 8*vo*. 10*s*. 6*d*. *net*. RAYMOND REVISED. *Crown* 8*vo*. 6*s*. *net*. RELATIVITY (*Fourth Edition*). *Fcap*.8*vo*. 1*s*.*net*.

Lucas (E. V.)
THE LIFE OF CHARLES LAMB. 2 Vols. £1 1*s*. *net*. EDWIN AUSTIN ABBEY, R.A. 2 Vols. £6 6*s*. *net*. VERMEER OF DELFT. 10*s*. 6*d*. *net*. A WANDERER IN ROME. A WANDERER IN HOLLAND. A WANDERER IN LONDON. LONDON REVISITED (Revised). A WANDERER IN PARIS. A WANDERER IN FLORENCE. A WANDERER IN VENICE. *Each* 10*s*. 6*d*. *net*. A WANDERER AMONG PICTURES. 8*s*. 6*d*. *net*. E. V. LUCAS'S LONDON. £1 *net*. INTRODUCING LONDON. 2*s*. 6*d*. *net*. THE OPEN ROAD. 6*s*. *net*. Also, illustrated by CLAUDE A. SHEPPERSON, A.R.W.S. 10*s*. 6*d*. *net*. Also, India Paper. *Leather*, 7*s*. 6*d*. *net*. THE JOY OF LIFE. 6*s*. *net*. *Leather Edition*. 7*s*. 6*d*. *net*. Also India Paper. *Leather*. 7*s*. 6*d*. *net*. FIRESIDE AND SUNSHINE. CHARACTER AND COMEDY. *Each* 6*s*. *net*. THE GENTLEST ART. 6*s*. 6*d*. *net*. *And* THE SECOND POST. 6*s*. *net*. Also, together in one volume. 7*s*. 6*d*. *net*. HER INFINITE VARIETY. GOOD COMPANY. ONE DAY AND ANOTHER. OLD LAMPS FOR NEW. LOITERER'S HARVEST. CLOUD AND SILVER. A BOSWELL OF BAGHDAD. 'TWIXT EAGLE AND DOVE. THE PHANTOM JOURNAL. GIVING AND RECEIVING. LUCK OF THE YEAR ENCOUNTERS AND DIVRESIONS. ZIGZAGS IN FRANCE. EVENTS AND EMBROIDERIES. 365 DAYS (AND ONE MORE). A FRONDED ISLE. *Each* 6*s*. *net*. SPECIALLY SELECTED. URBANITIES. *Each* illustrated by G. L. STAMPA. 5*s*. *net*. YOU KNOW WHAT PEOPLE ARE. Illustrated by GEORGE MORROW. 5*s*. *net*. THE SAME STAR: A Comedy in Three Acts. 3*s*. 6*d*. *net*. LITTLE BOOKS ON GREAT MASTERS. *Each* 5*s*. *net*. ROVING EAST AND ROVING WEST. 5*s*. *net*. PLAYTIME AND COMPANY. 7*s*. 6*d*. *net*. "THE MORE I SEE OF MEN . . ." 3*s*. 6*d*. *net*. See also **Dolls' House (The Queen's)** and **Lamb (Charles)**

Lucas (E. V.) and Finck (Herman)
TWELVE SONGS FROM "PLAYTIME AND COMPANY." Words by E. V. LUCAS. Music by HERMAN FINCK. *Royal* 4*to*. 7*s*. 6*d*. *net*.

Lynd (Robert)
THE ORANGE TREE. THE LITTLE ANGEL. THE GOLDFISH. *Each Fcap*. 8*vo*. 6*s*. *net*. THE BLUE LION. THE PEAL OF BELLS. THE MONEY BOX. *Each Fcap*. 8*vo*. 3*s*. 6*d*. net.

McDougall (William)
AN INTRODUCTION TO SOCIAL PSYCHOLOGY (*Twentieth Edition, Revised*) 10*s*. 6*d*. *net*. NATIONAL WELFARE AND NATIONAL DECAY. 6*s*. *net*. AN OUTLINE OF PSYCHOLOGY (*Third Edition*). 12*s*. *net*. AN OUTLINE OF ABNORMAL PSYCHOLOGY. 15*s*. *net*. BODY AND MIND (*Fifth Edition*). 12*s*. 6*d*. *net*. CHARACTER AND THE CONDUCT OF LIFE. 10*s*. 6*d*. *net*. ETHICS AND SOME MODERN WORLD PROBLEMS (*Second Edition*). 7*s*. 6*d*. *net*.

Mallet (Sir C. E.)
A HISTORY OF THE UNIVERSITY OF OXFORD. In 3 vols. Illustrated. *Demy* 8*vo*. *Each* £1 1*s*. *net*.

Maxwell (Donald)
THE ENCHANTED ROAD. Illustrated by the AUTHOR. *Fcap*. 4*to*. £1 1*s*. *net*.

Maeterlinck (Maurice)
THE BLUE BIRD. 6*s*. *net*. Also, illustrated by F. CAYLEY ROBINSON. 10*s*. 6*d*. *net*. DEATH. 3*s*. 6*d*. *net*. OUR ETERNITY. 6*s*. *net*. THE UNKNOWN GUEST. 6*s*. *net*. POEMS. 5*s*. *net*. THE WRACK OF THE STORM. 6*s*. *net*. THE MIRACLE OF ST. ANTHONY. 3*s*. 6*d*. *net*. THE BURGOMASTER OF STILEMONDE. 5*s*. *net*. THE BETROTHAL. 6*s*. *net*. MOUNTAIN PATHS. 6*s*. *net*. THE STORY OF TYLTYL. £1 1*s*. *net*. THE GREAT SECRET. 7*s*. 6*d*. *net*. THE CLOUD THAT LIFTED and THE POWER OF THE DEAD. 7*s*. 6*d*. *net*. MARY MAGDALENE. 2*s*. *net*.

Masefield (John)
ON THE SPANISH MAIN. 8*s*. 6*d*. *net*. A SAILOR'S GARLAND. 6*s*. *net*. *and* 3*s*. 6*d*. *net*. SEA LIFE IN NELSON'S TIME. 5*s*. *net*.

Methuen (Sir A.)
AN ANTHOLOGY OF MODERN VERSE. 135*th Thousand*.
SHAKESPEARE TO HARDY: An Anthology of English Lyrics. 19*th Thousand*. *Each Fcap*. 8*vo*. *Cloth*, 6*s*. *net*. *Leather*, 7*s*. 6*d*. *net*.

Milne (A. A.)

NOT THAT IT MATTERS. IF I MAY. THE SUNNY SIDE. THE RED HOUSE MYSTERY. ONCE A WEEK. THE HOLIDAY ROUND. THE DAY'S PLAY. *Each* 3s. 6d. *net.* WHEN WE WERE VERY YOUNG. *Sixteenth Edition.* 169*th Thousand.* WINNIE-THE-POOH. *Fourth Edition.* 70*th Thousand.* NOW WE ARE SIX. Each illustrated by E. H. SHEPARD 7s. 6d. *net.* Leather, 10s. 6d. *net.* FOR THE LUNCHEON INTERVAL. 1s. 6d. *net.*

Milne (A. A.) and Fraser-Simson (H.)

FOURTEEN SONGS FROM "WHEN WE WERE VERY YOUNG." (*Eleventh Edition.* 7s. 6d. *net.*) TEDDY BEAR AND OTHER SONGS FROM "WHEN WE WERE VERY YOUNG." (7s. 6d. *net.*) THE KING'S BREAKFAST. (*Second Edition.* 3s. 6d. *net.*) SONGS FROM "NOW WE ARE SIX." Words by A. A. Milne. Music by H. Fraser-Simson. Decorations by E. H. Shepard.

Montague (C. E.)

DRAMATIC VALUES. *Cr. 8vo.* 7s. 6d. *net.*

Morton (H. V.)

THE HEART OF LONDON. 3s. 6d. *net.* (Also illustrated, 7s. 6d. *net.*) THE SPELL OF LONDON. THE NIGHTS OF LONDON. *Each* 3s. 6d. *net.* THE LONDON YEAR. IN SEARCH OF ENGLAND. Each Illustrated. 7s. 6d. *net.*

Oman (Sir Charles)

A HISTORY OF THE ART OF WAR IN THE MIDDLE AGES, A.D. 378–1485. *Second Edition*, Revised and Enlarged. 2 Vols. Illustrated. *Demy 8vo.* £1 16s. *net.*

Oxenham (John)

BEES IN AMBER. *Small Pott 8vo.* 2s. *net.* ALL'S WELL. THE KING'S HIGHWAY. THE VISION SPLENDID. THE FIERY CROSS. HIGH ALTARS. HEARTS COURAGEOUS. ALL CLEAR! *Each Small Pott 8vo. Paper,* 1s. 3d. *net. Cloth,* 2s. *net.* WINDS OF THE DAWN. 2s. *net.*

Perry (W. J.)

THE ORIGIN OF MAGIC AND RELIGION. THE GROWTH OF CIVILIZATION. *Each* 6s. *net.* THE CHILDREN OF THE SUN. £1 1s. *net.*

Petrie (Sir Flinders)

A HISTORY OF EGYPT. In 6 Volumes. Vol. I. FROM THE IST TO THE XVITH DYNASTY. 11*th Edition, Revised.* 12s. *net.* Vol. II. THE XVIITH AND XVIIITH DYNASTIES. 7*th Edition, Revised.* 9s. *net.* Vol. III. XIXTH TO XXXTH DYNASTIES. 3*rd Edition.* 12s. *net.* Vol. IV. EGYPT UNDER THE PTOLEMAIC DYNASTY. By EDWYN BEVAN. 12s. 6d. *net.* Vol. V. EGYPT UNDER ROMAN RULE. By J. G. MILNE. 3*rd Edition, Revised.* 12s. *net.* Vol. VI. EGYPT IN THE MIDDLE AGES. By STANLEY LANE POOLE. 4*th Edition.* 10s. *net.*

Ponsonby (Arthur), M.P.

ENGLISH DIARIES. £1 1s. *net.* MORE ENGLISH DIARIES. 12s. 6d. *net.* SCOTTISH AND IRISH DIARIES. 10s. 6d. *net.*

Raleigh (Sir Walter)

THE LETTERS OF SIR WALTER RALEIGH. Edited by LADY RALEIGH. Two Vols Illustrated. *Second Edition Demy 8vo.* £1 10s. *net.*

Reumert (Elith)

HANS ANDERSON AS HE WAS. Illustrated. *Demy 8vo.* 10s. 6d. *net.*

Smith (Adam)

THE WEALTH OF NATIONS. Edited by EDWIN CANNAN. 2 Vols. *Demy 8vo.* £1 5s. *net.*

Smith (C. Fox)

SAILOR TOWN DAYS. SEA SONGS AND BALLADS. A BOOK OF FAMOUS SHIPS. SHIP ALLEY. *Each,* illustrated, 6s. *net.* FULL SAIL. Illustrated. 5s. *net.* TALES OF THE CLIPPER SHIPS. A SEA CHEST. *Each* 5s. *net.* THE RETURN OF THE "CUTTY SARK." Illustrated. 3s. 6d. *net.* A BOOK OF SHANTIES. 6s. *net.*

Sommerfeld (Arnold)

ATOMIC STRUCTURE AND SPECTRAL LINES. £1 12s. *net.* THREE LECTURES ON ATOMIC PHYSICS. 2s. 6d. *net.*

Stevenson (R. L.)

THE LETTERS. Edited by Sir SIDNEY COLVIN. 4 Vols. *Fcap. 8vo. Each* 6s. *net.*

Surtees (R. S.)

HANDLEY CROSS. MR. SPONGE'S SPORTING TOUR. ASK MAMMA. MR. FACEY ROMFORD'S HOUNDS. PLAIN OR RINGLETS? HILLINGDON HALL. *Each* illustrated, 7s. 6d. *net.* JORROCKS'S JAUNTS AND JOLLITIES. HAWBUCK GRANGE. *Each,* illustrated, 6s. *net.*

Taylor (A. E.)

PLATO: THE MAN AND HIS WORK. *Second Edition. Demy 8vo.* £1 1s. *net.*

Tilden (W. T.)

THE ART OF LAWN TENNIS. SINGLES AND DOUBLES. *Each,* illustrated, 6s. *net.* THE COMMON SENSE OF LAWN TENNIS. Illustrated. 5s. *net.*

Tileston (Mary W.)
DAILY STRENGTH FOR DAILY NEEDS. *32nd Edition.* 3s. 6d. *net. India Paper, Leather*, 6s. *net.*

Underhill (Evelyn)
MYSTICISM (*Eleventh Edition*). 15s. *net.* THE LIFE OF THE SPIRIT AND THE LIFE OF TO-DAY (*Sixth Edition*). 7s. 6d. *net.* MAN AND THE SUPERNATURAL. 7s. 6d. *net.* CONCERNING THE INNER LIFE (*Fourth Edition*). 2s. *net.*

Vardon (Harry)
HOW TO PLAY GOLF. Illustrated. *19th Edition. Crown* 8vo. 5s. *net.*

Waterhouse (Elizabeth)
A LITTLE BOOK OF LIFE AND DEATH. *23rd Edition. Small Pott* 8vo. 2s. 6d. *net.*

Wilde (Oscar).
THE WORKS. In 17 Vols. *Each* 6s. 6d. *net.*
I. LORD ARTHUR SAVILE'S CRIME AND THE PORTRAIT OF MR. W. H. II. THE DUCHESS OF PADUA. III. POEMS. IV. LADY WINDERMERE'S FAN. V. A WOMAN OF NO IMPORTANCE. VI. AN IDEAL HUSBAND. VII. THE IMPORTANCE OF BEING EARNEST. VIII. A HOUSE OF POMEGRANATES. IX. INTENTIONS. X. DE PROFUNDIS AND PRISON LETTERS. XI. ESSAYS. XII. SALOME, A FLORENTINE TRAGEDY, and LA SAINTE COURTISANE. XIII. A CRITIC IN PALL MALL. XIV. SELECTED PROSE OF OSCAR WILDE. XV. ART AND DECORATION. XVI. FOR LOVE OF THE KING. (5s. *net*). XVII. VERA, OR THE NIHILISTS.

William II. (Ex-German Emperor)
MY EARLY LIFE. Illustrated. *Demy* 8vo. £1 10s. *net.*

Williamson (G. C.)
THE BOOK OF FAMILLE ROSE. Richly Illustrated. *Demy* 4to. £8 8s. *net.*

PART II. A SELECTION OF SERIES

The Antiquary's Books
Each, illustrated, *Demy* 8vo. 10s. 6d. *net.*
A series of volumes dealing with various branches of English Antiquities, comprehensive and popular, as well as accurate and scholarly.

The Arden Shakespeare
Edited by W. J. CRAIG and R. H. CASE. *Each, wide Demy* 8vo. 6s. *net.*
The Ideal Library Edition, in single plays, each edited with a full Introduction, Textual Notes and a Commentary at the foot of the page. Now complete in 39 Vols.

Classics of Art
Edited by J. H. W. LAING. *Each*, profusely illustrated, *wide Royal* 8vo. 15s. *net to* £3 3s. *net.*
A Library of Art dealing with Great Artists and with branches of Art.

The "Complete" Series
Demy 8vo. Fully illustrated. 5s. *net to* 18s. *net each.*
A series of books on various sports and pastimes, all written by acknowledged authorities.

The Connoisseur's Library
With numerous Illustrations. Wide Royal 8vo. £1 11s. 6d. *net each vol.*
EUROPEAN ENAMELS. FINE BOOKS. GLASS. GOLDSMITHS' AND SILVERSMITHS' WORK. IVORIES. JEWELLERY. MEZZOTINTS. PORCELAIN. SEALS.

The Do's and Dont's Series
Fcap. 8vo. 2s. 6d. *net each.*
This series comprises clear, crisp, informative volumes on many of the activities of life.
Write for full list

The Faiths: VARIETIES OF CHRISTIAN EXPRESSION. Edited by L. P. JACKS, M.A., D.D., LL.D. *Crown* 8vo. 5s. *net each volume.* The first volumes are: THE ANGLO-CATHOLIC FAITH (Rev. Canon T. A. LACEY); MODERNISM IN THE ENGLISH CHURCH (Prof. P. GARDNER); THE FAITH AND PRACTICE OF THE QUAKERS (Prof. R. M. JONES); CONGREGATIONALISM (Rev. Princ. W. B. SELBIE); THE FAITH OF THE ROMAN CHURCH (Father C. C. MARTINDALE, S.J.); THE LIFE AND FAITH OF THE BAPTISTS (Rev. Princ. H. WHEELER ROBINSON).

The Library of Devotion
Handy editions of the great Devotional books, well edited. *Small Pott* 8vo. 3s. *net and* 3s. 6d. *net.*

Little Books on Art
Well Illustrated. *Demy* 16mo. *Each* 5s. *net.*

Modern Masterpieces
Fcap. 8vo. 3s. 6d. *each volume.*
Pocketable Editions of Works by HILAIRE BELLOC, ARNOLD BENNETT, E. F. BENSON, GEORGE A. BIRMINGHAM, G. K. CHESTERTON, JOSEPH CONRAD,

GEORGE GISSING, KENNETH GRAHAME, W. H. HUDSON, E. V. KNOX, JACK LONDON, E. V. LUCAS, ROBERT LYND, ROSE MACAULAY, JOHN MASEFIELD, A. A. MILNE, ARTHUR MORRISON, EDEN PHILLPOTTS, MARMADUKE PICKTHALL AND R. L. STEVENSON.

Sport Series
Mostly Illustrated. *Fcap. 8vo. 2s. net to 5s. net each.*
Handy books on all branches of sport by experts.

Methuen's Half-Crown Library
Crown 8vo and Fcap. 8vo.

Methuen's Two Shilling Library
Fcap. 8vo.

Two series of cheap editions of popular books.

Write for complete lists

The Wayfarer Series of Books for Travellers
Crown 8vo. 7s. 6d. net each. Well illustrated and with maps. The volumes are :—Alsace, Czecho-Slovakia, The Dolomites, Egypt, Hungary, Ireland, The Loire, Portugal, Provence, The Seine, Spain, Sweden, Switzerland, Unfamiliar Japan, Unknown Tuscany, The West Indies.

The Westminster Commentaries
Demy 8vo. 8s. 6d. net to 16s. net.
Edited by W. LOCK, D.D., and D. C. SIMPSON, D.D.
The object of these commentaries is primarily to interpret the author's meaning to the present generation, taking the English text in the Revised Version as their basis.

THE LITTLE GUIDES

Small Pott 8vo. Illustrated and with Maps

THE 62 VOLUMES IN THE SERIES ARE :—

BEDFORDSHIRE AND HUNTINGDONSHIRE 4s. net.
BERKSHIRE 4s. net.
BRITTANY 4s. net.
BUCKINGHAMSHIRE 4s. net.
CAMBRIDGE AND COLLEGES 4s. net.
CAMBRIDGESHIRE 4s. net.
CATHEDRAL CITIES OF ENGLAND AND WALES 6s. net.
CHANNEL ISLANDS 5s. net.
CHESHIRE 5s. net.
CORNWALL 4s. net.
CUMBERLAND AND WESTMORLAND 6s. net.
DERBYSHIRE 4s. net.
DEVON 4s. net.
DORSET 6s. net.
DURHAM 6s. net.
ENGLISH LAKES 6s. net.
ESSEX 5s. net.
GLOUCESTERSHIRE 5s. net.
GRAY'S INN AND LINCOLN'S INN 6s. net.
HAMPSHIRE 4s. net.
HEREFORDSHIRE 4s. 6d. net.
HERTFORDSHIRE 4s. net.
ISLE OF MAN 6s. net.
ISLE OF WIGHT 4s. net.
KENT 6s. net.
KERRY 4s. net.
LANCASHIRE 6s. net.
LEICESTERSHIRE AND RUTLAND 5s. net.
LINCOLNSHIRE 6s. net.
LONDON 5s. *net.*
MALVERN COUNTRY 4s. net.
MIDDLESEX 4s. net.
MONMOUTHSHIRE 6s. net.
NORFOLK 5s. net.
NORMANDY 5s. net.
NORTHAMPTONSHIRE 4s. net.
NORTHUMBERLAND 7s. 6d. net.
NORTH WALES 6s. net.
NOTTINGHAMSHIRE 6s. net.
OXFORD AND COLLEGES 4s. net.
OXFORDSHIRE 4s. net.
ROME 5s. net.
ST. PAUL'S CATHEDRAL 4s. net.
SHAKESPEARE'S COUNTRY 4s. net.
SHROPSHIRE 5s. net.
SICILY 4s. net.
SNOWDONIA 6s. net.
SOMERSET 4s. net.
SOUTH WALES 4s. net.
STAFFORDSHIRE 5s. net.
SUFFOLK 4s. net.
SURREY 5s. net.
SUSSEX 4s. net.
TEMPLE 4s. net.
WARWICKSHIRE 5s. net.
WESTMINSTER ABBEY 5s. net.
WILTSHIRE 6s. net.
WORCESTERSHIRE 6s. net.
YORKSHIRE EAST RIDING 5s. net.
YORKSHIRE NORTH RIDING 4s. net.
YORKSHIRE WEST RIDING 7s. 6d. net.
YORK 6s. net.